TO FRAN
A GLIMPSE
INTO THE PAST

Tim Sou

Beating About the Bushes

Tim Sommer

INFINITY
PUBLISHING

Copyright © 2008 by Tim Sommer

ISBN 978-0-7414-4981-8

Published by:
∞INFINITY PUBLISHING

Info@buybooksontheweb.com
www.buybooksontheweb.com
Toll-free (877) BUY BOOK
Local Phone (610) 941-9999
Fax (610) 941-9959

Printed in the United States of America

Published November 2012

TABLE OF CONTENTS

BUSH LEAGUE

A professional sports association at the lower levels of minor league organization.

The term originated from the state of minor league fields that often were ringed with shrubs and bushes.

IN THE BEGINNING

It was great to live in a neighborhood with enough talent to put together two teams if all the right elements came into place. Ages weren't regulated, and there was no restriction as to how long our game might last. It could be from dawn to dusk in a cow pasture, without boundaries, in North Canton, Ohio. I was living with my grandparents because of mother's problems, but this meant nothing to me at the time.

First person up threw pebbles against bedroom windows to awake as many players as possible. Occasionally mothers would dictate who would be playing, but this was understood. Games were influenced by daylight or until we ran out of baseballs. When it was the latter, we stopped and knocked on doors asking for bottles that could be returned for deposit money. I even sacrificed my 1954 Cleveland Indian autographed ball, won for being the MVP of the Knothole League in Norwalk, Ohio, in order to keep playing one afternoon.

Our family had moved to Norwalk because dad started an insurance agency from the ground up, believing in himself and his ability to succeed. This gamble allowed him to break away from working as a supervisor in a commercial laundry with no prospect of advancement and an income that didn't match his goals.

I was the proper age for Little League but there was no team, only the Knot Hole League. The organizer was a Norwalk High phys ed teacher by the name of Harry Shadle. You couldn't be more than sixteen and any lesser age became a personal decision as to whether you wanted to join. Our field was that of standard major league dimensions, matching the pitching distance I was used to while throwing a tennis ball against grandma's porch steps. On sign up day I was looking upward at everyone since my personal profile read five foot nine and one hundred fifteen pounds.

There weren't enough adult volunteers to coach the teams so when word came I couldn't play; there was only one thing to do. My call was to Harry Shadle, telling him he had a manager even though I was just old enough to have a Social Security card in order to pick strawberries this summer. When I read a story about any youngster who displays virtuosity in his or her field at an early age, I better understand my internal drive at the time.

Discovering how to make the ball bend while throwing a tennis ball against grandmother's front porch steps was exciting. This throwing drill became so sophisticated; there would be a radio broadcast within my head providing a mental image of the game.

Backing into the middle of Pearl Court, approximating major league distance and throwing the ball over and over again, I allowed my imagination to take over. If I hit the front edge of the step it would produce a line drive coming toward me with various arcs. Catching a carom in the air was out, on the ground was a base hit and there were no walks. A fantasy runner would make me adopt a stance designed to keep my opponent close to the bag. If there were no neighborhood interruptions, this drill would last for eight or more hours. I was twelve with a drive that allowed me to play professional baseball in a few short years and since my fastball was freakish, word started to spread in small circles.

I read an article describing how Satchel Paige in his early years was so full of himself, he ordered his outfield to come and sit on the edge of the infield because he was going to strike out the side. I did the same in our game following this reading and had I been old enough to be at the same level of schooling as my opponents, there could have been a butt kicking in the future.

Mid game and dominating, I turned to my outfield motioning everyone to come forward. They responded slowly thinking their depth was too great. But due to my continuous waving it became obvious something was out of the ordinary and all three came sprinting at full speed.

I was able to slow their movement when I lowered both upraised arms, like a symphony conductor. They understood the signal and sat, not knowing what was going on, because no one knew what was in my mind but me.

My catcher was a fifteen year old, Don Zureich, the best athlete on our team and the only person able to handle my pitches. Unfortunately, he was left-handed and his glove was a first baseman's mitt since there were no left-handed catcher's gloves on the market at the time. Because I knew what I wanted to throw, we devised signals where I would give the indicator instead of him.

There was an adult managing the other team and he was going insane. Typical response for someone whose ego could be damaged in a normal setting but this was beyond the norm. After striking out the side with no one coming close to putting a ball in play, he melted into the corner of the dugout. Given my immaturity, there was no way for me to understand what had happened. Almost every professional athlete, in any sport, has some twist to this tale.

The smaller town of Milan, Ohio had an official, first year, Little League team that qualified for the post-season district tournament with an average group of players. The one thing lacking was strong pitching and one night my parents got a phone call asking whether I would pitch for their team. This was against the rules since I hadn't played one inning for them but more importantly, I lived outside their district. This didn't matter to whoever was in charge since they were excited about going forward with a program only one year old.

What a change it was to be throwing a baseball fifteen feet less than the major league measurements I had adapted to this summer. The greatest adjustment was for Milan's catcher who had the job of catching me for the first time, often appearing to have a boxing mitt on his left hand instead of a catcher's glove. The game was limited to five innings because of the ten run rule where if a team is ahead by this margin the embarrassment is over for the other guys. I struck out fourteen and the other batter tried bunting, but his attempt came back to me in the air.

Soon there was a protest and violations were discovered. No way for me to experience Williamsport and the Little League World Series, but it was a great measurement as to my abilities. From this point on, I became the big fish in the small pond. I was twelve years old without knowing there were larger ponds and bigger fish in the world ahead.

SOME THINGS WERE HARD TO UNDERSTAND

Our family unit had been put back together after my mother's stay in a mental hospital, but there were conflicts between us, often unexplainable. A love for music developed because of the need to block her ranting at the base of the stairs directly below my bedroom. I built a stereo, from Allied Radio, with enough power to provide a white noise blocking effect against her tirades. Periodically, I turned down the volume and only when there was silence would I come downstairs. Since dad was outside the home doing his best selling insurance, this was a scene unknown to him.

Mom was extremely intelligent but her schizophrenia caused problems that were unseen by the community. Classmates knew nothing about me and any hint of instability would have been the end to dad's insurance business. Without knowing anything about the complexities of this illness, I moved forward with the belief I was going to play professional baseball.

My only start in a North Canton Little League game resulted in a broken nose while trying to catch a ball in right field. Coach carried me off the field and waited for someone to come forward. I had to ride my bicycle home alone after the bleeding stopped, wondering for the first time, why there was no support. Even at this age, her alternate personality understood where I was headed and wanted to stop the progress.

The first opportunity for my parents to see me play in a professional game was in Appleton, Wisconsin. I was excited since the normal rotation had me starting a strongly promoted Sunday afternoon game. There were more than three thousand people in the stands and I could see both after every pitch since their seats were directly behind home plate about ten rows up. This particular game was to be my fifth win in a row, on the way to an 8-0 start. Personally, there couldn't have been anything better to bring us together as a family, until the seventh inning.

When I came out for warm ups I could see mom was absent from her seat but dad was eating a hot dog, having a beer, and talking to many fans around him. It was obvious he was enjoying telling others of our relationship and sharing in my success. Mom never returned to her seat for the rest of the game and only after completing the nine innings did I find out what happened to her. As the game progressed, her absence caused worry but was countered by dad's happy demeanor and lack of concern.

Mom had met the mayor of Appleton underneath the grandstands on her way to the restrooms. She spent the missing innings discussing the attributes of Appleton and why my father should move his insurance business to the Fox Cities area. There were a few congratulatory words from my father for the win after the game and they returned to their motel room. I went out on the town to celebrate and cry.

Dad had to accept mom's anger after admitting taking time away from calling on prospective clients one Wednesday afternoon. He had hidden behind a tree so I wouldn't know his presence, but his anonymity was lost during dinner. "That was a hell of a curve ball you threw to get that last guy". Immediately, there was an argument as to why he spent frivolous time watching me when he could have been more productive making calls on prospective buyers.

My goal was hard for someone of the Depression era to understand. Mom was second in her Akron high school class and tutored children of the Akron rubber industry moguls in Greek, Latin, French and Mathematics in order to provide money for the family. Grandmother sold her beautiful hair to be made into wigs. Years later I would understand why my mother was placed in the Massillon State Mental hospital because of a multiple personality disorder.

The night before her commitment I was comfortably seated among major branches of a maple tree in grandmother's front yard, reaching out to capture lightning bugs for my glass jar. Mom came running from the house demanding I come down. She grabbed a leg and yanked me to the ground. "I just talked to the devil and he says you are no good and going to hell"! Within seconds she was pulled away by dad, gone the next day with no explanation as to why. Half way through her stay in Massillon I was allowed a visit for five minutes.

The scene was much like that of the ward in "One Flew Over the Cuckoo's Nest". This was heavy stuff for a ten year old to absorb and figure out. The approach to the hospital was a quarter mile, winding road with beautiful trees and grass leading up to the entrance. The closer we got I could see, but not understand why; there were bars on all the windows. Mom's image had almost faded from memory but there still was the want to see her. Dad had to hunt through grandmother's house before finding my secret hiding place in a bedroom walk in closet and we could make this trip.

During the thirty minute ride little was said between the two of us since our family had been torn apart for a long time. The only positive reinforcement during the period of separation came from my grandparents and what baseball offered. This combination supported me during difficult times.

The first person I saw at the hospital was a middle-aged man sliding down the curved stairway banister leading to the second floor where my mother was housed. He was dressed in a drab uniform and offered, "Whee!", and a wave as we passed. To me, he was just having the kind of fun I would be enjoying if left alone.

7

The second floor was the waiting area that also served as a large day room for the patients. We were told there would be a short wait. I watched thirty people doing many things, which didn't seem normal, such as the person facing into a corner reciting the alphabet over and over. The daredevil on the banister repeated his fun many times before we were led down a corridor.

Mom's room was that of a jail cell. There was a small cot, nightstand, and a stainless steel toilet and sink. She was seated on the side of the cot, rarely raising her head or voice while we visited. My dad prompted conversation since I didn't know what to say. It wasn't possible for me to know or understand she had been going through electric shock therapy and only recently had been evaluated by staff allowing our contact.

Psychiatric opinion of the time was a patient had to be awake during this non-lethal electrocution. Today it is recognized benefits can be achieved while sedated, but memories of this treatment carried over to the last days of her life.

Her eventual release from the hospital provided little time for me to grasp what was ahead. I only knew we were going to be together once again and the comfort of my grandparent's home would be missing. There were to be six more years before I could leave mother's influence behind.

There were constant conflicts between the two of us that often didn't make any sense. Even though I had natural athletic ability, playing high school basketball was not possible because of mom's order to work after school. Dating was forbidden even though I had developed feelings towards Lois Wilkinson. The only time she and I were together was our senior year when I won an argument about going to the senior prom. My leverage came from being a class officer and the embarrassment if I weren't to attend the dance.

TIME TO MOVE ON WITH LIFE

Ohio University was my college of choice for several reasons. I had been selected by the Norwalk teaching staff my junior year to be our representative to attend Buckeye Boy's State at the university. This is a yearly gathering of several thousand students in an accelerated governmental atmosphere creating a functioning state structure during our two-week stay. You could run for office or wait for appointment by the winners. I chose to wait and was awarded a position overseeing bovine registrations. The natural beauty of the campus nestled in the hilly southeast corner of the state made me comfortable and it was far away from home.

Events leading up to moving into a dorm room are a blur. My roommate was a last minute concession because we were from Norwalk. Chuck Carpenter and I were the only males to choose OU and were now forced to tolerate each other in a ten by twenty room for the next year. Chuck was serious about his education and I could care less. Not being allowed to play high school sports or have a date produced a sorry individual to have as a roommate.

Had I been allowed to experience life in high school as Chuck had, I know we would have been good friends and might have helped prevent the waking of our dormitory area one night. It was two am and the bars couldn't serve me anymore when I pointed my speakers out the window. This was to provide culture for all to enjoy by cranking "The William Tell Overture" at max volume.

Early on I realized I didn't have a chance in the Chemical Engineering degree program my mother chose for me. Rejecting her decision would have resulted in my not going to college. While chemistry came easy at the high school level, I didn't have a clue as to what the next step required. Advanced math was a weakness and foreign languages were impossible. My intelligence testing level had reached a zenith when I nailed a 1300 in the SAT's. I chose German since the only other language to take was Russian and I'd have to learn a new alphabet. I flunked the class but won the award for the best accent due to all the World War II movies I loved to watch.

One January afternoon I walked into the Convocation Center looking for the head baseball coach. The first person I asked pointed over my shoulder and said, "There's Coach Wren now. If you hurry you can catch him before he leaves". With that, I sprinted fifty feet and placed myself in front of this person so he couldn't advance.

"Coach Wren, my name is Tim Sommer and I'm going to come out for the baseball team this spring"! Bob Wren didn't say anything, but took careful inventory of the person in front of him. Six foot one, one hundred thirty eight pounds, wearing black horned rimmed glasses with lenses so thick they bordered on being labeled as "Coke bottles". "That's nice son, I'll be looking forward to seeing you on the field". Not one question as to my background or how I got there. I had been given a polite brush off by one of the most respected baseball coaches in NCAA history who now has the stadium at OU named for him.

I was late finding the room for freshman sign ups and had to take a standing position at the rear. After the coaching staff made introductions, a legal pad was circulated with pages to sign up by position. I was the twenty sixth pitcher to register but the large number didn't cause panic. In my mind, they were all country bumpkins like me. I just knew I was better than all of them and though my pond had grown larger, I was still the big fish.

There were no indoor training facilities as there are now. You just showed up the first day of practice and tried to survive. I had secretly maintained the conditioning of my arm by sneaking into the Convocation Center late at night, throwing a tennis ball at a wall, much like I did against grandmother's porch steps in North Canton. I was ready.

Our first day of practice in March was held in near freezing temperatures with a light mist in the air. Since we had so many pitchers, position players were forced to catch us and the scene was comical. They were trying their best to make the team and couldn't say no to the coaching staff. The poor soul assigned to me was a second baseman with a glove that had seen its better days and was trying his best to catch a ninety plus mph fastball without breaking his hand.

Empathy is defined as identification with and understanding of another's situation. Sympathy is a feeling or an expression of pity or sorrow for the distress of another. I had both in my heart, but my goal was to throw heat and that I did.

Coaches were patrolling the line and one could feel their presence when they stopped. None of us were throwing from a mound. We were distributed along a foul line and flinging baseballs from somewhere around sixty feet. One coach had approximated the distance after pacing much like a golf caddy. Coach Wren stepped forward from the group and tapped me on the shoulder.

"Son, have you been throwing this winter? It's pretty early to cut loose like this and I don't want you to hurt that arm". I'm positive he didn't tie together the two different images that had been offered to him; the skinny kid in the Convocation Center and the one in front of him coming straight over the top with a rising fastball.

"Coach, I've been throwing indoors all winter with a tennis ball and my arm feels great." "Do you have a curve"? I nodded my head and turned to face someone whose eyes were showing genuine fear. He went into a semi crouch because there was no way for him to gage the drop of the ball or speed.

11

Due to the nature of my build, I was able to bend my wrist at a ninety-degree angle at the top of my motion and pull downward with my fingers gripping the seams. This means maximum velocity and a baseball traveling towards the batter that appears to be straight but at the last minute "drops off the table."

There are many euphemisms for this pitch and I think my favorite was the "yellow hammer". What the heck did this mean and where did it originate? Old time coaches would yell this during the course of a game and all would know what it meant, except the average fan. To me, this was much like code talking by Native American's who baffled the Japanese during Word War II.

My yellow hammer was on the way and instantly I knew it was a good one, even without the added leverage of a mound. The perfect pitch was when there was so much rotation my first two fingers would come into contact with my thumb, producing a click. My catcher never had a chance. He started with his glove upright but didn't have enough time to react to the drop and took the hit off his right shin. There was no experience in Orville or wherever he came from to compare. Coach Wren watched him walking away and said to me, "Son, take a shower and come see me in my office".

Bob Wren was interested as to how I flew under the baseball radar, arriving on his doorstep totally unknown. Over the next hour he understood as I described having to play during the summer in semi-pro games for the Sandusky Soldiers and Sailor's Home around north central Ohio. He did have a hard time understanding why Norwalk High School did not have a spring baseball team like everyone else. This was a question on my mind prior to my senior year and without my parents or any of my friends knowing, I appeared unannounced before the school board one night.

Since I knew money for uniforms and equipment would be the biggest objection, I spent the previous month putting costs together and, more importantly, found money for a startup program. Without knowing what I was doing, I had prepared a business plan and was ready to go. It didn't matter to me that each uniform would have a different sponsor's name along with the high school nickname of "Truckers". I thought it would be cool to see "Norwalk Auto Body" on someone's jersey.

"Truckers" came from Norwalk Truck Lines, which was a large carrier in the Midwest until being bought out by Yellow Freight. A major contribution to my efforts came from the founder, John Ernsthausen, but I was sworn to secrecy as to the money source if the program was approved. He would write me a check and then I would be writing my own check to the school board. As I remember the deal, it was for more than half of the startup costs. We shook hands in the middle of his back yard while I was mowing the grass. He was my next-door neighbor and he really liked me.

My turn before the board came and I was nervous, but not afraid. This was the same feeling I had before my first pro start. In the five minutes allotted, I laid out a logical plan for the addition of a major sport to Norwalk High's athletic program without any cost to the taxpayers. Apparently this was too logical for the board members this particular night. There wasn't even a huddle to get opinions and maybe table the request until the next meeting. The board president delivered the death sentence.

"While your presentation has merits, we feel it would not be in the best interests of Norwalk High to approve your request. There are many other factors you are obviously not aware of for a program such as this. One of the most important, in our minds, is this will potentially take away athletes from our other spring programs and dilute the talent". The only spring programs I knew of were golf, tennis and track. If you went out for the first two you were ridiculed for playing "sissy sports" and the track team had been near last for ten years in the Northern Ohio League. Half of this team wanted to play baseball in the spring and keep on going during the summer. I knew when I was licked and there probably wasn't even an inclusion to the minutes of the meeting about my proposal.

Life changed dramatically after my successful freshman year when Bob Wren awarded me a full scholarship. This meant there were no educational costs, not even for books. Now, I had the leverage to approach my mother about changing majors. There would be few worries about parental support and I could really do what I wanted.

I thought my mother would be proud of what I had been able to do on my own, but was dead wrong with this assumption. Any deviation from her plan was unacceptable and produced another strain on our relationship, carrying over to the one person whose support I needed, my father.

Since I was forced to attend summer school in an effort to raise my GPA, coach Wren arranged for me to pitch for the Logan, Ohio entry in the Hocking Valley Association. Teams in this league were part of very small communities tied into the coal mining regions. Fans worked the coal six days a week and came to the games on Sunday ready to enjoy one of the few pleasures afforded them.

All the infields were uncertain due to small lumps of coal that inevitably worked their way to the surface causing interesting bounces. Sometimes games had to be halted to allow dairy cows to return to the barn for milking as their path went directly through the outfield and always, there were fresh pies left in their wake. One time a fly ball fell into the middle of a deposit and our outfielder refused to reach in and soil his hand. This was the only inside the park home run I ever saw caused by such a circumstance. I've always wondered how the official scorer in a professional game would have ruled this night.

The locals were incredible for their fervor and support and several times we had to leave a field armed with bats since we won over their team. Often I would look in for my catcher's signal and see someone climbing the screening with one hand while clutching a quart Pabst Blue Ribbon bottle in the other. They did love their baseball.

In order to return to college my sophomore year, a complete separation from my family had to occur and, fortunately, there were angels following me in the form of Joe and Eunice Russakov. They were the parents of my best friend and had been my moral support through my formative high school years. They didn't hesitate when I asked for a $500 loan in order for my return to college with the scholarship support. When I signed my initial $2500 bonus check from the Orioles I went to a bank, purchased a money order and paid my debt.

I had a note in my mailbox to see Coach Wren privately in his office. This scared me greatly since my world was on shaky grounds because of problems with my parents and also academics. My mind had almost locked up when I walked into his office. "Tim, I understand what you have been going through and I've made an arrangement to help you out. I don't want to lose you to our program and I think you are about to turn the corner. This is something between you and me and nobody else can know. There isn't another player I've done this for".

Coach Wren then gave me a slip of paper with an address of a commercial laundry on the other side of Athens and I was to report the following day for work. This came from a coach who also oversaw the collegiate career of a Hall of Famer, Mike Schmidt, and a future major league manager, Bob Brenly.

What had been "arranged" was a job starting at 4:45 pm and a finish at 5:00 am. The catch was, I left five minutes after the office closed at five and the night janitor clocked me out in the morning when he left. Every Friday I backed up to my paycheck with a smile.

Even though I had been advised to keep this quiet, I had no idea it was illegal according to NCAA guidelines. To me, this was an act of charity from someone who was a father figure and genuinely concerned about my well-being. It wasn't until I made a trip up to Ohio State to visit a high school friend, Bob Middaugh, did I learn about the illegalities.

Bob was truly the star athlete our senior year at Norwalk, eclipsing Mark Fowler. Both achieved All State rankings in their respective sports. Middaugh in basketball and Fowler in football and we three came together in Chemistry class taught by Mark's dad. Marcus Fowler looked the other way when I tilted my test papers for Bob to copy from. As much as I didn't have a chance at the college level to understand chemistry, Bob wasn't able to look at a recipe in the Betty Crocker Cookbook and make any sense of it. But his jumper from the corner was deadly, attracting interest from many Division I colleges.

Ohio State thought enough of Bob's talents to award him a full scholarship in basketball for the 1961 season. This was exciting to me since he would be part of the varsity inner circle, which included John Havlicek, Jerry Lucas and Larry Siegfried. State had won the NCAA championship the previous year and now I might possibly be able to rub elbows with some of my heroes.

Larry and I had competed against each other this summer in baseball and it was fun for me to kick his butt in my sport. All three went on to careers in the NBA and it was awesome when I had the chance to join everyone in their frat house when I visited Bob. There was no reason for Middaugh to visit me in Athens so I went to Columbus as often as I could. Always, it was via the hitchhiking route since I didn't have a car or extra money.

The most unusual transportation came the day a car pulled over outside of Athens during my second trip. "If you're going to Columbus, hop in". The two in the front seat seemed normal until we got back on the road and our car approached 100 mph. The driver was most interested in telling me about their cargo and wanted to know if I wanted some.

"Just haulin' some shine up from our still. Big demand at State. All them young kids can't afford the good stuff so we pop up and sell what we got out of the trunk. This shit is really good. My grand daddy started our operation during Prohibition and we're keepin' it alive". To me, this was like listening to the ancestors of the Jack Daniel line describing their product with the same pride. We slowed to the speed limit outside Columbus and even though I was riding in a vehicle piloted by two people who had been passing their product back and forth for an hour, they agreed to play taxi and drop me off at the frat house.

"Anybody in there who wants a good deal"? After telling them everyone was involved in advanced mathematic degree programs and probably wouldn't want any, we parted with hearty handshakes. My last memory is that of the opened trunk. Inside were more than 200 bottles heading to other parts of campus.

Since my "secret" deal with Coach Wren was now in place it wasn't a matter of conversational importance initially. Bob introduced me to everyone as "my best friend from Norwalk who has one hell of a fastball". Soon I was hanging out and shooting the breeze with the All Americans.

When Bob and I had a chance to be alone, I told him about the laundry arrangement at school and his eyes got wide. "You haven't told anyone about this have you"? After I assured him I hadn't, he clued me into the rules and regulations of the NCAA and how I could be kicked out of school if this infraction were discovered. He then went on to tell how it was done at Ohio State.

"There are alumni who take a player out to dinner on a regular basis during the course of the year. The bill might come to forty dollars and they'll hand you two or three hundred to pay and you keep the change. Unless there are NCAA spies at the particular restaurant, nobody will ever find out". To me, this seemed far less risky than what I was involved in. I would leave the laundry through the back door which opened into an alley and if there were anyone in sight, I would wait until they left. Paranoia had already set in.

Bob called once inviting me up for a weekend since he had landed a gig playing piano for a prominent patron of the arts in Columbus. Our transportation to this person's home was on a small motorbike with Bob dressed in his tux. We were joined at the hip when it came to jazz and it was beyond my comprehension how he could do what he did, completely self taught.

There were late afternoons our senior year when we would skip classes and go to his house listening to records, always leading into Bob playing incredible, improvisational music. His facial expressions showed me he really wasn't in the room, but somewhere else in his mind as he created music worthy of recording. At this party I found myself sitting on a staircase alone with one of our heroes, Cozy Cole, while Bob played.

Cozy was one of the greatest jazz drummers of all time having played with the likes of Louis Armstrong, Cab Calloway, Lionel Hampton, Gene Krupa and even recorded with Jelly Roll Morton in the '30's. He appeared in a number of films including, "The Glenn Miller Story" in which he played a duet with Krupa. Cole also broke many of the racial barriers in music when he became the first black musician on a network staff. CBS hired him to work with Raymond Scott in 1943. In 1958, he had a surprising double-sided hit single in Topsy I/TopsyII selling more than a million records and reaching the Top 40 in mainstream rock and roll.

I couldn't resist asking a question that must have been asked a thousand times over. "Cozy, how did you get your nickname?" I watched his face to see the reaction and maybe the need to get up and move on, saving myself a lot of embarrassment. The smile that formed and the look in his eyes told me I had pushed the right button.

"That's a great question and I can't remember the last time anyone thought to ask. I guess I've been around music for so long, everyone just accepts the name and maybe thinks my momma just hung it on me. When I was young, I loved to play basketball and my style of play created an expression in our neighborhood. 'Man, look at the cozy way that cat handles the ball'." When Bob finished his set, Cozy and I applauded from our private spot and went our separate ways.

This was the last time Middaugh and I were together and our sporting careers took a different path. Bob suffered a terrible knee injury requiring multiple surgeries, and without the techniques available today, his career was over without realizing how far he might have gone.

Fortunately, he had the opportunity to experience the ultimate level in sports through his daughter, Tuesday. She was a member of the 2000 Olympic team in synchronized swimming and Bob shared the moment with her in Australia before his passing several years later with throat cancer. I would trade many memories to hear him play once again as he did this last night with the endorsement from Cozy Cole.

All of Coach Wren's efforts were for naught since my college life style was too ingrained. Even though I had switched to psychology and Chuck and I had parted as roommates by mutual agreement, I was doomed. The grades weren't there and I had to work through a difficult period upon returning home until the opportunity from Baltimore changed my life.

Many years later Coach Wren and I had a chance to reunite after taking my daughter to the Ohio University campus for her freshman year. Chris chose this school mainly because her best friend in life, Jenny Scholl, had been awarded a scholarship for swimming and another Elmiran,

Trevor Thomas, was on campus under scholarship playing baseball due to my efforts. There were tiny aftershocks felt on campus after my brief stay, but they were there to feel.

Ohio University was the leading "party school" in the MAC and there were temptations everywhere you turned. Matt Lauer, NBC's current morning anchor had a few of these problems facing him during his collegiate experience but he was too young to experience the turmoil on college campuses during the Viet Nam era.

A most famous photograph was taken on the Kent State lawn after a National Guard member shot and killed a student, one of four killed that day. The image was a young girl cradling the head of the victim and looking skyward with a silent, questioning scream as to why this had happened. Few people know Ohio University was the most radical campus in the state at this time and could have been the backdrop for the same tragedy.

Given my success at the professional level I was curious as to what might have happened if I had been able to return to OU refocused on academics. Coach Wren didn't hesitate in his analysis and reinforced my own thoughts.

"You would have been number two on the staff your sophomore year and number one the next. If you were successful, I would have pushed for All American recognition your senior year. The 1964 Olympics in Tokyo reintroduced baseball as a sport for consideration and I know you would have had a shot at that team." This knowledge was extremely gratifying since Bob Wren was the only person I could turn to in making my decision when Baltimore made an offer.

I had failed miserably at academics and was operating a die cutter in a cardboard factory punching out Crest toothpaste boxes making $2.25 an hour. This was even below wages made at the fake laundry job on campus. I picked up the phone and called Athens. Terms of the simple contract were being discussed when coach Wren stopped the conversation.

"Tim, as much as I would like to have you back in the program you must understand how few players have this opportunity in life to fulfill a dream. The money isn't as important as moving to the next level and finding out whether you are good enough. I tried and it wasn't there for me. If I convinced you to turn this down and something happened to you physically here at OU, I would feel terrible. My advice is to go forward and give it your best".

"I just talked to Coach Wren and I'm going to sign with Baltimore". My mother turned and walked away and my father was non responsive since any positive reaction would have serious repercussions. He had to live with her for many more years after I left. I was going to escape soon but he couldn't. My life settled into a daily routine that was numbing until I signed the contract and left for spring training.

PROFESSIONAL VALIDATION

In some ways it was hard to imagine the day had come when I realized my dream to play professional baseball and signed a contract. It wasn't earth-shattering news, but to me, this was the equivalent of being elected President. The only people present were my parents, Ken Meyers, a reporter and photographer from the Sandusky Register. Ken was the Baltimore scout who had enough belief in me to push Baltimore into my signing.

Our local paper, the Norwalk Reflector Herald, didn't deem this to be much of a story and sent nobody to cover the event. It wasn't until the Register ran a large feature story did anyone from our paper want to know details as to the signing. In a way, this was fitting, because everyone in Norwalk had looked at me as a dreamer having zero chance of ever being a professional baseball player.

The only Norwalkian to reach the major leagues was Hank Edwards. He started his career with Mansfield in the Ohio State League in 1939 and finished playing for Austin in the Texas League in 1956. In between, he played for five major league teams including the pennant winning team of the Cleveland Indians in 1948. He led the American League in triples in 1946 and actually received two votes in the Hall of Fame balloting in 1960.

An irony surfaced a couple of years ago when Don Hohler tracked me down in Arizona and collaborated on a story for a magazine published in Ohio. Don was the resident reporter for the Reflector when I signed and given the chance to be there in my home that day, didn't show up. His article was good and sparked an interest in our small community resulting in phone calls, letters and postcards from all parts of the country.

There was some humor as the photographer jockeyed everyone around the dining table. He eventually had me hold the pen in my right hand rather than my natural left hand. This was the only way he could get everyone in the picture making sense to the lead paragraph, which would say, "The right hander from Norwalk". There was concern readers would assume an error had been made by the paper and the negative had been reversed. Once everything was over, I walked out of the house without saying a word and went on to do something planned from the minute I became a professional.

Lefty Grove, a Hall of Fame pitcher, lived close by on Parson Street with his son, Robert Jr. I don't know exactly when he moved there but I was aware of his presence and importance. Walking down the street I was in a fog and had no conscious plan of what to do or say when I arrived at his doorstep. I was on the same professional level as this famous person and for all anyone knew, my career could equal or exceed his credentials in due time.

Now I was standing on the front steps of a small, well kept, ranch house and my objective was straight ahead. I pushed the doorbell and almost turned and ran until the realization sank in, there was no turning back. Maybe Lefty wasn't home or, he was hard of hearing in his latter years and had become a recluse.

The door opened slowly and I was looking upward at someone who appeared to be approaching seven feet tall. I hadn't done any research about the person and didn't know Lefty was six feet four. Adding the extra inches from the doorsill to his height made him appear to be a giant. I had to say something and it came out in one long sentence in a high-pitched voice that didn't seem to be coming from me. "Hello Mr. Grove, my name is Tim Sommer and I just signed a contract with the Baltimore Orioles and I wanted to come say hello to you". I took a step backward and waited.

"Hello son. Would you like to come in for some cookies and tea and we'll talk about our careers?" This was like walking into the Hall of Fame at Cooperstown and having a guided tour from one of the most famous members there. I can't remember how I responded, but shortly I was sitting on a living room couch awaiting the offerings and wondering what to do next.

I didn't have to wait long nor worry about what to say, as the next hour was all Lefty's. It was like he had waited a long time for my visit just to tell his stories over again. I listened to tales of playing against greats like Ty Cobb, Babe Ruth, Lou Gehrig, and others. They were names that had made up my dreams ever since I was able to understand the pull and drive within to play this fantastic game. Most of the time his gaze was focused elsewhere and I knew he could see the people and events as he described them to an audience of one.

There reached a point when Lefty looked at his watch and declared, "I'm sorry, you're going to have to leave now. I have to get supper ready for my son; he'll be home soon. Come back after your first year and tell me all about it. I'm very interested in how you do." I never made it back because, like all young people, I became too involved with myself knowing there would always be time in the future to go visit this wonderful old man and spin my tales.

When I returned home I found my mother upset since I hadn't shared where I was going. When I explained I had gone to see Lefty Grove, she reacted as if I had gone to play in a mid afternoon poker game with a shifty guy by the name of Lefty. Once again, my dad had a smile on his face but offered no help in my defense. Typical parental reactions, but there was no way anyone would rain on my parade this day.

I WAS HARD TO BELIEVE

After signing my first contract, the Orioles sent a questionnaire asking for physical details and this request for verification came via telegram from Baltimore's farm director, Harry Dalton.

Dear Tim:

Is your weight correct? Stop. If so, see family doctor. Stop. Get on weight gain program.

Stop. See you this spring. Stop.

Regards,

Harry Dalton

I learned years later from Harry, they wanted to fire the scout who signed someone six feet, one and one half inches, weighing 145 pounds. It was damning for the scout since they had given me several thousand dollars signing bonus without any cross check by another scout. Four years later I would learn how I became a small legend on my own.

Mom and dad were coming to see me play in York, Pa., and I was standing at the box office window in full uniform making sure tickets were there when a cab pulled up. The passenger was someone in his sixties, supporting his walk with a cane, addressing me directly. "Son, are you Sommer?" "Yes sir, I am."

This person identified himself as a scout for the Pittsburgh Pirates. The team I rejected in the bonus bidding process even though they would allow me to play for Columbus at the AAA level to finish the season. Since there was no information available as to talent levels at this time, I chose Baltimore's offer as the only way to mollify my mother.

"I want to ask you a question." To me, it was obvious his intent was to find out if I wanted to join the Pirates organization via a high level, multi-player trade since I had thrown a three hit shutout against their York club in my first start of the season and he had been there.

"Is it true you ate four complete chicken dinners in a sitting one spring training? I'm sure you aren't aware of stories about this skinny kid who showed up at camp and couldn't stop eating everything in sight. I just want to find out for myself if maybe there has been exaggeration over time." It took some time to move away from this question and respond. "Yes sir, it's true.

The weekly visits to Dr. Camardese during the winter had produced a monster incapable of controlling the urge to eat. There were injections with unknown substances weekly and several prescriptions taken daily, all focused on increasing my appetite and caloric input. Even though I averaged six to eight milkshakes a day, along with the food, I gained a total of four pounds. After the first week of spring training all the weight gain was gone leaving doubt as to my future. What wasn't lost was the ravenous appetite and it became a game to make sure I wasn't the lightest person in the camp of almost two hundred.

There was a second baseman from Puerto Rico who was my closest challenge when we weighed in every Monday morning prior to practice. We watched each other's measurement by our trainer much like that of prizefighters. I never lost this contest, because he didn't come to the cafeteria early enough to see me eating six bananas, a double breakfast of scrambled eggs and, my newly found favorite food, grits.

My legendary dinner was four halves of chicken with all the accompanying offerings, mashed potatoes, biscuits, coleslaw, beans and dessert. I was out of control because of the drugs I had been taking and the next day there was no weight gain. I was a freak, much like Steve Dalkowski, able to throw a baseball with great velocity without the expected appearance of a professional baseball player.

Ron Guidry became my hero when he was picked by the Yankees in the third round of the 1971 draft. It is doubtful his statistics of 5' 11", 160 pounds were accurate, especially the weight. This was probably padded by ten pounds since no organization would admit to taking this chance and most baseball scouting personnel felt he was too small to pitch effectively and survive in the major leagues.

Guidry proved them wrong by going 16-7 in his first full year with the Yankees and went on to lead the major leagues in victories from 1977 through 1987 with 168. He is fourth on the all time Yankee victory list (170), second in strikeouts (1776), sixth in games, innings pitched and shutouts. He won the Cy Young award in 1978 with a record of 25-3 and an ERA of 1.74.

In 1975, Ron left AAA Syracuse mid season, frustrated with both his performance and the lack of support by the Yankees. Only a few hours into the trip returning to his roots of Louisiana, his wife delivered an ultimatum totally opposite of most wives in baseball. She demanded he turn their car around and return to Syracuse because she didn't want to be married to a quitter.

Watching Guidry's success was my gratification since a scout from the Cincinnati club told my parents that new directives had just been issued and no pitcher would be signed under the height of six foot three. This was offered in the stands after I had pitched a shutout in the Ohio National Baseball Congress game with sixteen strikeouts. Even though my club didn't win the championship, the winning club was allowed one at large selection to go to the national tournament and I was their pick.

DIFFERENCES BETWEEN NORTH AND SOUTH

When I saw rural Georgia for the first time the cultural shock was hard to measure. Nothing I had ever done prepared me for what was immediately ahead. Looking back, this was one of the most important time periods of my life, providing guidance as to the way I look at people and their diversities.

The train left Bellevue, Ohio on a dull day in March headed somewhere so far from Norwalk only my imagination could produce images. My mother believed this was running away in order to avoid responsibility for growing up. My father was prideful but we only shook hands before boarding. It wasn't until many years later, standing in our kitchen in Elmira that we ever shared this moment. Once this happened, the floodgates opened and with tears and hugs we established a bond that should have been there years before.

My destination for the first leg of the journey was Washington, DC arriving early in the morning. Typical for transportation of this era, there was an eight-hour layover before heading to Georgia. Thinking I would never return to this city in a lifetime, there were things to do and see. It was going to be difficult as there was only $125 in my pockets but, somehow, I would find a way.

Near the railway station was a lineup of cabs and I selected a driver who looked younger and less threatening than the rest. "Please take me to the Washington Monument," He turned around and took a long time responding. "Where you from"? This was one of the few cab rides I had ever taken and scared to death of losing all my money in some form of scam. With much bravado I responded, "Norwalk, Ohio". A broad smile broke out on his face and he said, "Yeah I know where that is, I got a cousin who lives in Huron." I had now made a friend and it was going to be a great day.

It turned out my cab driver was a friendly person with more problems than I could imagine. He had lost his job and had a couple of kids who recently had been ill, resulting in large doctor bills. Driving a cab was the only way to immediately make money for his family and not lose his personal sense of worth.

We were in motion when my driver made a proposal. "For forty bucks, I'll take you anywhere you want to go for the next four hours and won't run off and leave. How's that?" Since I had made an investment in this guy, I took him up on the offer and looked on it as an opportunity I might not be able to recreate.

Straightaway we went to the Washington Monument and I got out wondering whether to look back over my shoulder to see if he had driven off. I chose to move forward showing confidence he would keep his word. After about fifty steps upward in the narrow passageway of the memorial, I reversed direction believing this to be a waste of time and effort. I walked into the sunlight and saw my friend waiting by his cab smoking a cigarette.

We hit many of the high spots, Lincoln Memorial, Arlington Cemetery, the Capitol and Iwo Jima Memorial. There was still a little more than an hour left and we were trying to decide where to go next. "Want to see a really neat place?" I was open to any suggestion at this time. "Yeah, wherever you want to take me." We sped off to an unknown destination.

The cab pulled up to a large building that had few markings. There was an even bigger building across the street with absolutely no identification. He had brought us to the printing office where all our currency originated and the other building was where all old money was burned. This stop turned out to be the highlight of the day.

29

I was able to hook up with a tour of the printing facility quickly. We were led onto catwalks spreading over the lower level where printing presses were spitting out various denominations as fast as the machines could cycle. A surprising thing was most workers operating the presses were black and contrasted with our white female tour guide.

Off to the side were inspectors going over sheets for printing errors and they were all white. In total, there must have been 300 people busy making all this money. I focused on presses spitting out $100 bills and after reaching into my pocket there was recognition as to just how poor I was at that moment.

Our tour concluded with the guide asking if there were any questions. After a couple of vanilla responses from our group, I raised my hand. "Do you have any psychological problems with the workers handling all this money?" There was a noticeable pain to her expression as she answered with, "I don't know what you mean." To me the question seemed obvious.

"I was just wondering how people resist the temptation to somehow slip away with some of the money. I'm sure they're like everyone else with bills to pay." My cab driver's situation is what made me think of this as I saw millions of dollars floating around the floor. "No, we never have problems like that!" she answered emphatically. But, as we were walking back to the tour starting point, she touched my arm and motioned me aside.

When everyone was gone she said, "I've been a tour guide for ten years and no one has ever asked that question. Yes, we do have this problem and constantly have to be on the alert." I couldn't admit to her I probably would be one of those problem employees if I worked there.

The allotted time with the cab driver was over and he dutifully returned me to the train station as promised. It had been one of the best experiences of my young life and the day seemed to have lasted a week with all we had done. My future was ahead and about to explode because I was going to spring training as a member of the Baltimore Orioles family.

My first train trip was to play in the National Baseball Congress tournament in Wichita, Kansas the previous year. But it couldn't compare to this ride south and my first camp. The scenery was always changing outside the window and I didn't have the distraction of the hell-raising going on the entire time during the Kansas trip. At night the moon was almost full and try as I might, I couldn't fall asleep despite the even rhythm of wheels crossing the steel rail ends. Never in my life had there been such a feeling of being totally alone.

After breakfast, and for most of the day, I got to know our conductor quite well. He had the appearance of someone my father and grandfather had described for years during their weekly Sunday dinner table discussions about railroading. Both were avid railroaders and the fried chicken dinner always ended with both of them throwing out initials of rail lines both current and defunct in an attempt to stump the other. Surprisingly, my father held his own against the older expert.

As we progressed into Georgia, there was a decided change in the look of the land and people we saw. The dirt took on a red hue and the people had an aura of poverty. We were cutting through this state where there were no major roads and no population centers to speak of when a scene shocked my senses.

I was standing in between cars talking to the conductor when our car passed a black family standing next to the tracks. There were at least eight people and the very young were wearing no clothes. As we passed, they stood motionless and only started to move away from the tracks after the last railway car had gone by. I asked the obvious question of the conductor, "What are they doing by the tracks?"

He responded with, "Everyone along this route knows the schedule of all passenger trains and they come out hoping our dining car will throw off garbage as we went by. This would go a long way toward helping to feed the family. It's sad isn't it?"

I had nothing to draw upon for a response, as it was impossible to understand what had just been seen. At the least, it helped prepare me somewhat for my next forty-five days in Thomasville. But there was no warning about the cross burning in the front yard of a farm on our return one night from a night game in Waycross. Cal Ripken was the driver and I was in the front passenger seat. No one in the car said a word as we passed the scene.

The final shock of the trip occurred as we pulled into the station. The train slowed, allowing a sign to scroll before my eyes much like today's news headlines on television. I read and reread the message trying to comprehend, "NO SPITTING ON SIDEWALK BY COLOREDS ALLOWED". Below the sign were two drinking fountains. One was labeled, "colored" and the other was "white". One had not been cleaned for months and the other was gleaming white. This carried over to the public restrooms nearby.

SCARED TO DEATH

Our training facility was a state Veterans Hospital outside of town that had excess capacity and rented the facilities to Baltimore. The unique aspect was there were four fairly good baseball fields to use and Baltimore was able to gather more than 150 players in one location in order to evaluate talent.

The only teams not there were AAA Rochester and the major league club. Our living quarters were wings branching off a long hallway in an area fairly distant from the residents. Each wing housed about thirty players and had a private room for a coach to oversee the tightly wound people under his supervision, sometimes proving to be an impossible task.

The most curious part of the housing was black players were separated from the white players by four barracks. We ate in the same cafeteria and played on the same fields, but there was a degree of separation every night when we went to sleep. This arrangement had been in place for years and only ended in 1965 when integration arrived without fanfare at our barracks.

We reported this year to find bunks had been assigned placing everyone together for the first time. This made sense since many close friendships were formed over previous seasons and no reason for separation. We just couldn't do anything together outside our temporary home because this was the South. Most radio stations signed off at midnight and it wasn't the national anthem played, but some rendition of Dixie. The South was going to rise again but we would be long gone before this would happen for any of us.

Most frightening to me was the number of players who, by their own self promotion, seemed head and shoulders better than I ever thought of being. The first night I went into town with a couple of these studs while trying to get my bearings. The weather was warm and contrasting to any early March evening in the north. The fragrant orange blossoms shocked me and became something I looked forward to each year.

Our first stop was a drug store with a soda fountain providing a connection to Norwalk. The layout was exactly the same as that of Walgreen's during high school and there was a young high school girl working behind the counter. I wanted to say something but nothing came out and the longer this pause went, the more awkward it became. Finally, I grabbed a pack of gum placing it front of this southern beauty. She rang up the sale returning my change and in a smooth, syrupy drawl offered, "Y'all come back and see me again, ya heah?'

No one had ever said anything to me like that or in that way. I tried to figure out how to ask for a date since she was obviously impressed with me. Reality set in when she turned to the shelves and started dusting with a feather duster, completely ignoring me. This was my first experience with the communication gap between North and South.

Soreness from the first days of training had worn off and a sorting of friendships took place. Several of us started going to the downtown area for R&R each afternoon. It was interesting to try and blend with locals, but proved to be impossible. We might as well have been branded with a "Y" on our foreheads for Yankee.

There was one particular bar a few of us always gravitated towards during our afternoon visits to town. It was centrally located and in one of the oldest buildings around. When you entered it was like stepping back in time in more ways than one. The obvious was dark wood all around with a patina that only results from undisturbed aging. The less obvious, until you spent some time within, were the characters inhabiting this place every afternoon. The faces changed slightly each day but all possessed a common thread tying them together. It was their age and an unbelievable penchant for playing what I called the "Civil War Game". This scene did not change for the three springs I spent in Thomasville.

I soon realized they were grandsons of men who actually fought in the Civil War and stories told were words I had read in textbooks. History was coming to life in front of me in the form of men repeating family stories told at their dinner tables. Their own daily strategic twists as to how lost battles could have been won gave them pleasure.

While most of my buddies didn't pay attention to their ramblings, I eavesdropped as often as possible. I don't remember trying to insert myself in their war games because there was nothing for me to contribute. There was a feeling it might disturb the fragile relationship we had with this group. They accepted us because we had some hint of fame but knew we were intruders and non-believers as to their cause.

One day I was at the bar by myself and had the opportunity to listen in on one of the verbal chess matches. An old timer sporting a huge gray beard was giving a detailed analysis of a strategic move during a particular battle. It was as if he were actually returning from the front and going through debriefing.

"If Lt. Carpenter had moved his artillery to the top of the hill this would have stopped that dinky group of New Yorkers from flanking his outfit. This turned out to be the weak point in the line and caused the eventual retreat. In my opinion, this was the turning point of the battle and if we had held, it would have caused General Lee to reconsider his next move."

I left the bar that day never forgetting what had been heard. This probably did more for my understanding of the deep division between North and South than anything else. Even more than seeing the burning cross in the front yard of a home or a continuing debate as to whether the confederate flag should or shouldn't be flown in public places.

This camp produced one of my least proud moments in life. We were separated by more than one hundred yards from the main facility where veterans were housed, producing a false sense of isolation. Many of these gentlemen were from World War I with no family and they attended our daily games with great enthusiasm. Typically, there were never more than one hundred people in the stands and the veterans stood out.

One character in particular would show up and remove his wooden leg, placing the appendage at his side. When the moment was right, he would start pounding the leg on the seat next to him offering advice for the hitter along with observations about his life. My favorite was, "I come from somewhere so deep in the South, they have to pump sunshine in"! His voice was distinctive and had we both been in Memorial Stadium with fifty thousand people cheering, we would have connected easily.

Word quickly spread that many of the California players had bought large amounts of fireworks on their trip to Thomasville. The southern portion of the country sold these explosives to anyone with a dollar and they had loaded up. Once the action plan started, it was amusing to watch the extra oranges taken from the cafeteria each day. These would be hollowed out and fitted with a "cherry bomb", which had the power of a quarter stick of dynamite.

There was no coordinated time for an assault between barracks, but when it happened, everyone was prepared and oranges were tossed over roofs exploding with a loud concussion and no concern about possible harm. This was a bunch of fun until the authorities arrived with lights flashing and it wasn't only local police, but state since we were on their property.

No one considered the emotional impact for the veterans. Many reverted to their war experiences, calling for extra ammunition while hiding beneath beds. Several completely locked up emotionally resulting in months of therapy to understand what had happened. Somehow, the Orioles took care of this night, but the following year we were elsewhere for spring training.

CULTURE SHOCK

The first trip to Thomasville produced sensitivity to a racial slur never heard while growing up in Norwalk. The word "nigger" was something that occasionally came up in movies but never in my everyday life. In our community I can only remember two black families, the Woods and Oglvies. I am sure there were others, but these were the people in my classes. Thomasville was no different than any other city or town in the South; it just provided my introduction to this offensive word.

One day, at my favorite bar, one of the regulars turned and yelled out, "Hey nigger, get over here and give me a shine!" From a dark corner never noticed, a young boy about nine or ten, came running up to the patron. He had a small stool, a box with cans of polish, rags and a well-worn brush. "Yes boss, I give you a real good shine." I watched this action to see if there would be anger for having been called "nigger" or an air of superiority by his employer. There was nothing I could sense and wondered why this young person wasn't in school learning there was a potential better way of life.

Visual observations of Thomasville offered contrasts everywhere you went since there seemed to be no middle class. Beautiful mansions with Georgian columns and well-manicured lawns were within sight of wooden shacks that hadn't seen a coat of paint in decades. Grocery stores catering to blacks had hams hanging outside with insects crawling on or flying around them.

Signs of segregation were everywhere and everything seemed to be in a loop for the three springs I spent in camp. Nothing changed, including the slowness in finishing any project. One year there was a simple brick arch entrance to the city placed into construction and the following spring it

time. Craps and the fast paced action eluded me and I relegated this game to a time later in my life.

The sophistication and beauty of the hookers around the high rollers was something to observe. Because they were out of my league, the possibility of enjoying these pleasures never crossed my mind. I was innocent in these matters and would have had a heart attack if someone accepted an offer. But our second trip of the year brought a different animal to town.

Now I knew how to play their games. My speculation at the tables was minimal but, in my mind, I was equal to the biggest spender they had any given night. I knew how and when to tip, when to accept the complimentary drink designed to get you off your game and all this in only one month.

During a late night wandering I discovered a "sports book" in the rear of Harrah's. The sports book now is a big element of the gambling scene, but in 1963 it was relegated to an obscure corner away from the hard-core action. What fascinated me was an old, dusty chalkboard listing every game in the California League for the next day. Obviously, they wouldn't know the starting pitchers so it was a straight bet. There it was. Stockton vs. Reno.

I backed away to the safety of a slot machine and measured my next move. I knew, even at this early stage of my career, gambling on baseball was illegal even if Baltimore hadn't advised any of us it could be career ending. We were expected to pick up this information on our own, much like sex education. Finally I stepped up to the betting window but went mute. It was three am and I couldn't engage my brain.

"What's your pick?", asked the person handling my action. At this point, I knew my choice but not how much to bet. Now I was trapped and instead of answering in the proper sequence, I just put a twenty in front of him and stood there grinning. "Well, who do you want?" It was obvious my stupidity was wearing thin with someone who didn't enjoy the night shift away from his family. I almost screamed, "Stockton!" He turned to look at the board. To me this was bigger than anything going that night and once the bet was made, I became brazen.

"Do you know who the pitchers are tomorrow?" "Nah, I never go to the games, I don't like baseball." This set me back only for a second and I resisted telling him who he was dealing with. The easy thing would be to forfeit. The walk back to the hotel was comforting because this was the surest bet I would ever make.

The following night I pitched a complete game winning easily and the fun began. I can honestly say the wager never entered my mind before or during the game. But afterwards was a different story. The urge to tell someone was intense but the fear of being found out was greater. All I had to do was walk into the club and collect these easy winnings.

While walking towards Harrah's the realization of what I had done took over. The thrill of winning was gone, replaced by the original worries when placing the bet. Suddenly, everyone I looked at appeared to be an agent of professional baseball out to nab me and end my career. The easy thing would to be to forfeit my winnings, but this was countered by the accomplishment and the competitive nature kicked in. Somehow, I had to collect and enjoy the short-lived euphoria of a professional win both on and off the field.

I went from club to club trying to build courage before arriving at the casino. Working my way to the rear I glanced at each player, every dealer and pit boss to see if they were watching. No one seemed to be, but I couldn't be certain. To make sure there were no baseball spies around, I took up a strategic position at a nickel slot with a view of the sports book. After thirty minutes I felt secure enough to collect the bet.

Stepping up to the window, I handed over the ticket looking left and right. I must have had the appearance of a bank robber, but the attendant casually handed me two twenty-dollar bills and off to the hotel I went. Since I still wasn't totally convinced of having pulled this off, my route back led me down back alleys that could have produced disastrous consequences.

I was in far better shape than one player, several years later, who hid in his closet for a day after being caught slipping extra money onto a winning blackjack bet while the dealer finished other players. When security started closing in, he bolted to the safety of his room and didn't come out for the game. He was convinced if he appeared before a window there would be someone from security watching.

This poor soul had been signed by Baltimore after being discovered playing in a rural area of Virginia. His education had stopped at the third grade level in order to work the fields to assist in the support of a large family. His talent was seen on Sundays playing for a semi pro team possessing the live arm all scouts look for.

What none of us knew was he couldn't read or write. Something was wrong when autographs had several letters missing from both his first and last names, which were lengthy. The answer came mid season when someone questioned why he ordered fried chicken every time on the road when a restaurant menu didn't have pictured food. His father had given him parting advice that no matter where he went, every eating place would have fried chicken as a fall back meal.

Years later, when Pete Rose was banned from baseball's Hall of Fame for gambling, my experience and memories came back strongly. I had done something that went against the fiber of professional baseball. The only thing that could have been more damning would have been placing a bet to lose that game.

Pete stupidly placed bets with a bookie directly from the clubhouse phone. Several friends were to play with Rose in the majors and described Pete Rose as one of the most ignorant persons they ever met. Proof positive you don't have to be intelligent to play this game well.

Pete has now admitted to placing bets on his team in a confession he believes will further his chances for Hall of Fame admission. This comes after countless interviews denying the same. This secures my belief about post humus admission as the only option for voters.

Quite often, when people learn of my background, an opinion is solicited as to whether the ban is fair to Pete. There can be no arguing as to his credentials, but like me, he knew the rules and chose to break them. My good fortune was not getting caught.

GAMBLING 102

1966 brought me back full circle to the league where my career started. The cause for this was political and worth discussing separately. Once again I was in Reno and little had changed from before. This time I stayed away from the sports book and concentrated on blackjack. Like all bettors at some time in their lives, I had developed a "system" for winning. Of course this had to be kept secret, so I went alone into the city after checking in to my room.

The bus didn't leave the hotel until five and there was time for testing my system on the tables. When I arrived at the park there was an additional $200 in my jeans because the system had worked and there would be no more money worries for the rest of my life.

In the bullpen, where all pitchers are expected to absorb knowledge from the game, I couldn't figure out how to handle the winnings. Finally a logical conclusion came to mind. I would stay in my room this night and the next day turn cash into something tangible, like a good sport coat. It was a great game plan but poor execution on my part followed.

On every road trip there was a poker game to be found with players drifting in and out all night long. Usually, the game lasted until four or five in the morning and bets limited to nickels or dimes. This allowed minimal damage to one's pocket book while providing Type A personalities additional competition. Many would sleep until mid afternoon, eat something light and be ready for the game.

This night I joined the action, surprising most players since I hardly ever played in these games. My strategy failed early because the window of our room was wide open and casino sounds couldn't be avoided. My card playing was terrible because I couldn't concentrate and it was time to revisit the "system" once again.

I left the game and returned to my room retrieving a single twenty from my stash. The winnings had been hidden behind the radiator stuffed in a sock, not to hide from my roommate but from myself. This would be my limit and if there were profits from planting this single seed, I would multiple my wealth even further. If there was a loss, there was enough to pocket and declare myself a winner.

Our hotel had a small casino and I knew there was a beautiful dealer on duty this night. I headed straight to her table and was surprised to find all the seats were open. Her nametag told me she was Allison from Alabama. "How ya'll tonight?"

There it was again, that sexy, smooth, southern drawl designed to draw the unsuspecting player into her web. Within fifteen minutes my twenty was gone but I was hooked by her allure, returning to my room to get another bill. Over the course of the next two hours, I made eight more trips wearing a path in the carpeting.

"Ya'll have just had the worst streak of luck I've seen in quite awhile." I couldn't tell her this big time gambler in front of her was busted and his system had been flushed. I quietly left her table dragging myself back to the room without a whimper.

We were blessed this season with a general manager who refused to give us our paychecks if playing Reno was in the immediate future. He protected married family income and all of us from our own stupidity. No one complained about this arrangement until our final trip of the year.

The last series was against Reno and after our return everyone would have a fresh travel voucher for airfare from Stockton to their place of residence, as listed in the Baltimore files. Those who knew the system would gamble during contract negotiations. The further away from one's listed home address versus the season ending city, monies would be greater. There were many who used brothers, sisters or girl friends for their addresses. Sometimes they won this game and sometimes they lost.

A small committee went to the park early in the afternoon two days before departure to convince our GM everyone's checks should be released. After haggling for an hour we won out. Since paychecks were so highly personal, there was no way to tally the amount we collectively had put together for the trip. The figure turned out to be more than $10,000. Everyone went his own way and, oddly, there wasn't a single mention of winning or losing by anyone for the first two days.

We went about our evening jobs of playing ball and regrouped each day in the hotel lobby before catching the bus to the park. Still, it was strange when no one would offer the question, "How'd you do?" Even the spacing around the lobby said something was amiss since friends who normally would join up stayed apart and alone. On our final day the truth came out.

Starting about noon, the request of, "Hey, how about lending me five bucks?" became the standard question and spread like wildfire. It soon became clear every player, manager and bus driver had lost everything. Once we joined each other in misery, stories of how when and where surfaced becoming a badge of courage to describe details surrounding a loss. This slaughter took place in little clubs and big clubs. The games of chance covered the gamut of what was available and the end result was, we all were busted.

As we were getting closer for departure to the park, realization set in no one had any money to buy their dinner. Since we wouldn't arrive in Stockton until early morning the next day, panic set in. Someone came up with an idea on how to keep all of us from starvation.

All players squirrel away change in their shaving kits over the course of the season as a matter of convenience rather than necessity. Suddenly, all twenty-five were opening up their luggage in the middle of the hotel lobby and raiding these kits for whatever monies they would produce. Guests checking in and hotel staff looked at us like we had collectively gone mad at the same time.

We pooled our money on a large table and started counting. It turned out there was enough to buy bologna, bread, mustard, chips and pickles for the entire team. I'm sure the hotel was quite upset with the picnic that ensued in their lobby but we didn't care. The Stockton Ports had staved off starvation and would live to play another day.

After the game, our route out of town took us back through the center of Reno. A player sitting directly in front of me, a soul mate linked to all our losers, jumped up and pulled down the top window. Screaming as loud as he could and scaring everyone, he offered, "I'll be back to get you sons of bitches!" With that release he slumped into his seat and the bus continued on. I doubt he ever made good on that promise but it would be a great story to tell his grandkids.

THERE WERE NO STEROIDS

The 1960's were an extremely explosive period in our history producing a deep division between leaders and youth of this country. The Vietnam War was viewed by many as being senseless and catalyst for change in many areas. Music shifted overnight from rock and roll to songs of protest.

Rioting in the streets was seen by the world to be illustrative of the "Ugly American" and memories of this carry over to this day in many countries. The use of drugs turned from experimentation with marijuana to hard line addiction. The demographics of our prison system changed also and drug offenders increased dramatically as they continue to do so with moral, legal and economic questions.

I can honestly say for the years I played (1963-1970), I only witnessed the usage of "greenies". Drug usage wasn't even mentioned in inner circles and there were no veiled references either. The sport of baseball seemed to be insulated as far as I could sense, though living in California several off seasons made me aware of how much the general public was participating.

The term for the pills came from the color of the most commonly prescribed diet pill on the market at the time. Today this is known as "speed" and abused by many. Most clubhouses in 1969 had a direct source and ours in Elmira was no exception. Almost always any club's supply came from the team's doctor.

It was viewed as a performance enhancement for those who burned the candle at both ends, fitting the description of most professional athletes enjoying life to the fullest without regard to their future. I had no intention of ever taking greenies until an all night adventure caused me to reconsider. There was no way I would be able to stay awake for the entire game and it would have been embarrassing to fall off the bullpen bench.

Secretly, I slipped back to the clubhouse unseen by going underneath the right field stands. Since it was mid game I could go directly to the large glass jar where the pills were kept, out in the open for all to use. The recommended dosage was two but since I was near collapse, four seemed more appropriate to solve my problem. The return trip to the bullpen took less than two minutes, but I could feel the drug's effect taking over.

Our field lights started increasing in intensity as my pupils dilated and it became impossible to sit for more than a moment or two. I started pacing back and forth from one end of the bullpen to the other just as big cats do in a zoo. This drug lived up to the reputation as everything sped up around and within me.

Suddenly, the signal came to start warming up because our current pitcher was in trouble and I was going to be in the game. There were no telephones at this level so hand signals were required. Mine was hands raised with thumb and forefinger placed together indicating round eyeglasses. It was normal for me to take only a few pitches to get loose and this night was no exception. Harry Bright summonsed me and I came running at full speed. This should have been a tip off since I always walked in from the pen.

Harry handed me the ball and returned to the dugout totally unaware of what he left standing atop the mound. When I finished warm ups there was no doubt in my mind I was the fastest pitcher ever to play the game, including Steve Dalkowski. There was a question as to why my catcher hadn't gone back to the locker room for extra padding in his glove.

The first signal was for a breaking pitch but that didn't suit me. The next was for a fastball and this was what I had been waiting for. I wound up and threw a pitch that should have been leaving vapor trails, it was thrown so hard. The batter took a swing and pulled the ball out of the park foul. This had to be a fluke since nobody could get his bat around fast enough to do what he had done. I repeated the pitch with the same results.

My mind now understood what was happening and I struggled to pull myself together. There was real fear as to what this drug had done to my thinking and coordination. Somehow I got through the inning with no damage to the score or myself and made a vow to never try this again. This was a promise I kept and no one ever knew what I went through this night.

Fred Kendall was our primary catcher and would go on to an average career in the big leagues. His son, Jason, is enjoying a lengthy stay in the major leagues at the same position with much more success.

Kendall was outgoing, good looking, and partied hard. He also was exception to the rule about all of us congregating together on the road. Fred slipped into the night without leaving a wake, many times being delivered to our hotel in the early morning hours by a beauty. Everyone was jealous and wanted more details but Fred never talked about his trophies.

We were playing a Sunday doubleheader in Williamsport, Pa. with temperatures and humidity approaching 100 degrees. Fred was the catcher in the first game and would not be catching the second. Unfortunately, our second catcher, playing another position, went down late in the game with an injury and Kendall was faced with putting the gear on once again. All hell broke loose when he learned this.

Williamsport had a very old ballpark and clubhouses were below the stands. To get to the field, one had to walk a circuitous path underneath before reaching the dugout. I was returning to the field when I heard an angry discussion building between Fred and our trainer, Bob Jones. It seems "Jonesy" had forgotten to pack the greenies for this trip and once Fred found out he was without his crutch he went out of control.

"Listen Jonesy, there's no goddamn way I'm catching this second game unless you come up with some greenies. I don't give a shit whether you forgot them or not, just come up with something!" Having heard this ultimatum, I turned the corner and found Bob in a rage. I considered Jones to be a good friend of mine and I knew he resented the cocky, arrogant attitudes he had to face on a daily basis. To his credit, he handled all personalities with the skills of a degreed psychologist.

I asked, "What can I do?" "Nothing, I know how to handle this asshole!" With that, off he went to the Williamsport clubhouse and came back shortly with a small bag of greenies, enough to handle Fred's crisis and possibly others. It seems the Williamsport trainer owed Jonesy a favor from his previous trip to Elmira. Fred caught an excellent game and our trainer was off the hook.

"Ball Four" was a bombshell book published in 1970 setting the precedent for tattletale writing within sports. The author, Jim Bouton, was a veteran pitcher picked up by the expansion Seattle club after a career pitching for the New York Yankees.

His book chronicled a major league season for the first time from an inside perspective giving the average person an accurate and shocking insight into the abnormal life of a professional athlete. There were no punches pulled and many heroes were shown not to be the deities created by the media, but human beings with many faults. This was accomplished without any of his teammates having knowledge since Jim kept notes on a small notepad and, when questioned as to what he was doing, offered evasive and bizarre explanations.

When "Ball Four" hit the market, everyone I knew rushed out to buy. It was interesting from our perspective because anyone who had been in the game a few years could identify with situations or actually know one or more of the players Bouton had written about.

I noted early in the book a mention of greenies and their use by the Seattle players. Bouton said the club was running low and since management had denounced them, the supply had to be shipped in by players from other organizations. I was cruising through the book astounded to be reading all the inside tidbits. Then, on page 211, I became involved.

"At dinner Don Mincher, Marty Pattin and I discussed greenies. They came up because O'Donoghue had just received a season supply of 500. "They ought to last about a month," I said. Mincher was a football player in high school and he said, "If I had greenies in those days I'd have been something else." "Minch, how many major-league players do you think take greenies?" I asked. "Half?, More?" "Hell, a lot more than half, he said, "Just about the whole Baltimore team takes them, most of the Tigers, most of the guys on this club. And that's just what I know for sure." There it was out in the open for all to see.

John O'Donoghue was a vain person who never let anyone forget his status as an ex-major leaguer. It didn't matter he never had a winning record in the bigs for any club. He had been in the "show" and don't you dare presume he wasn't worthy. Somehow, he had landed in the Orioles organization in 1968 and been assigned to Rochester in 1969.

Greenies were not available in the Rochester clubhouse but we had our own importer in the person of Al Severinsen. Al was from New York City with a connection for stolen pills. One night, just before we were to take the field for batting practice, O"Donoghue gave Severinsen thirty dollars for 500 pills with an agreement their arrival to be in a couple of weeks. Minutes after this transaction our manager, Cal

Ripken, came out of his office to inform John his contract had been purchased by Seattle and he was to leave immediately to join their club somewhere on the road. The last words we heard as he left were, "Hey Al, don't forget to ship me my greenies!"

Several weeks later, Severinsen received a large box in the mail and inside were the recent orders placed by players on our club. Since Al was a man of honor, he would comply with O'Donohue's request to forward his narcotics and this is where I came into the picture.

Al didn't own a car and asked if I would give him a ride to the post office the next day to forward the shipment. By this time I had the feeling this greenies thing was getting risky. I asked, "Don't you think this is something dangerous to do?" "Screw him! I won't put any return address on the box and it's his problem if something happens when they arrive." That satisfied me. Off to the post office we went and a year later there I was, vicariously, in Bouton's book.

A PROFESSIONAL PERK

"Baseball Annies" is a term coined by Jim Bouton in his book, "Ball Four". Later, the more popular tag was "groupies" and associated mostly with the music business. References were meant to describe females who are attracted to professional performers for no other reason than their fame.

In every city there were women who came to games and taverns with the express purpose of meeting a ball player and a goal of going to bed with him. Word of mouth spread during spring training as to the hot spots and continued into the season. Quite often, conversations between opposing players prior to each game concentrated on this very issue.

Final days of spring training are interesting once rosters are set and there is a need to collect information about each city in the league. The ultimate prize was to come up with an out of the way place with the best female to male ratio that only a few knew about. This knowledge would help filter and reduce the competition and I needed all the help I could get.

Our first trip to Clinton, Iowa produced a pleasant surprise and was my first experience to the Baseball Annie situation as described by Bouton. The previous year, being my rookie year, I was stumbling around trying to find my way with the fear of being released always on my mind. But once this season was over and I realized there was a semi-solid foundation to my career, I blossomed. Now I could look around and enjoy the scenery without any overriding influence from my mother.

We won the first game of the series and came into the locker room full of ourselves, whooping and hollering like we had won the seventh game of the World Series. I hadn't pitched that night but was caught up in the excitement like everyone else, except for the guy occupying the locker next to me. He was silent and starting to dress without taking a shower. I knew him slightly from spring training but never before saw this rejection of personal hygiene. I whispered so as to not bring attention to his actions.

"Aren't you going to take a shower?" He didn't say a word and put a finger to his lips to indicate silence. He motioned to follow him to a remote corner of the clubhouse. We stood on benches to look out a small window facing the dimly lit parking lot of the stadium. There, about a dozen figures could be seen moving about our team bus. It was so dark their gender could not be determined, but my mentor knew. The shadowy figures were from Mt. Saint Clare College, an all girl school.

A large portion of the student population came from the east coast being placed there by wealthy families unskilled in parenting. To provide punishment and discipline, they were shipped to the middle of nowhere knowing their strict rules and curfews at this Catholic college.

As we walked up to the group I could see prospects varied widely. The range was from painfully homely to stunningly beautiful and the closer we got panic set in. How do you play this game? Constantly scanning the faces of our dedicated ladies produced a match. One girl looked at me and her face produced a smile that lit up the parking lot. I had to change course to get to her position since she was standing far enough apart from the main group to raise the question as to whether this attractive person was available.

Reaching out, I touched her arm pulling her further away from the group. Once we achieved separation, it became easy to get to the heart of the matter. Each girl came with a blanket, a bottle of wine, transportation and a need to be back to the college by curfew. Though I have had no experience with a hooker, our rapid conclusion to the act must be similar.

The girl I selected was from Connecticut and her father owned a small record company in New York City. Neither parent had spent any time or effort in her upbringing. She hungered for friendship but was facing exile in the middle of the cornfields of Iowa. Holidays were the only permitted trips home.

The sexual aspect of the relationship actually diminished and our brief time together each night was spent in philosophical discussions about our lives. At the end of the season there were no tears, only a mutual respect for each other and the joy we shared in knowing each other.

The first time I heard the name "Chicago Shirley", was 3am at the Brown Hotel in Louisville, Kentucky and came from my roommate. We both had been sound asleep and the ringing phone scared the hell out of both of us. "What?, holy shit, we'll be right up." From the tone of his voice and excitement I could only imagine a team meeting had been called to announce the entire Rochester team was called up to replace the Orioles. "Come on, get your ass up. Chicago Shirley's in the hotel." When I didn't respond immediately he quickly gave me a briefing as to what this was all about.

"Chicago Shirley" was a schoolteacher from the Chicago area who had a goal to give sexual favors to professional athletes in every sport. Time off during summer months apparently allowed her to reach out and cover the top minor leagues and she was here in the middle of the night in Louisville.

"Bullshit. I'm not going anywhere tonight." With a shrug of his shoulders off went my roomie to sample Shirley's delights. I vaguely recall his returning to the room slipping quietly into bed without saying a word or attempting to wake me. Either the experience didn't live up to the expectation or he viewed me as a threat to tell his wife. The following day in the clubhouse there was no discussion of the event between anyone.

SOMETIMES YOU NEED TO BE HUMBLED

Without knowing what was ahead, 1964 was going to be an incredible year for me. This included the brief relationship with a hitchhiker I picked up somewhere in Georgia along the way to spring training. Since his makeshift cardboard sign read, "Daytona Beach or Bust", he must be a college student heading for fun in the sun and I felt it my duty to give him a lift. There were few worries in this era about personal safety and a wonderful way to meet someone on the road.

My passenger was an engineering student from Georgia Tech who decided at the last minute to take off on his own for Daytona Beach. In the next few hours we shared many thoughts about life as if we had known each other for years, rather than minutes. He understood my forsaking college to do something he secretly longed to do and I felt good about his drive to get a degree. Almost a decade later we were to be reunited.

Mary and I had just moved into our first home In Elmira when the postman delivered a letter with no return address. Inside was a major article from the Baltimore Sun describing a visit by the Orioles team to a military hospital in Oakland, housing wounded from Viet Nam and the interaction between players and combat soldiers.

"A wounded Captain, whose left leg was blown away by a land mine, asked about an Orioles farmhand who gave him a lift to spring break one year. Someone went to find Harry Dalton and bring him to this soldier's bedside".

"I've always wondered how this "kid" ended up in baseball. We really hit if off when he picked me up hitch hiking and he even went out of his way to get me to a road that would get me to Daytona. I thought a lot about him in 'Nam since he just didn't look what I thought a pro baseball player would look like, but I am curious as to whether he survived". Harry provided details as to my career and assured him I was doing well in Elmira, NY.

I couldn't resist picking up our phone and calling the hospital mentioned in the article. I anticipated layers of resistance in trying to reach this person, but once I gave an honest reason for the call, governmental blockades disappeared. I had touched a nerve with those who had grown to know him and why there was a need to say hello once again. They provided his home telephone number somewhere deep in the hills of Kentucky.

The person who answered my call said, "He just came in the front door, let me get him. I think I know who you are. Are you the guy in the article"? Once I assured her I was one and the same, my traveling partner came on the line. There were fifty people in his house for the homecoming, but he took my call.

We shared ten minutes of conversation with most of the questions coming from him as to my professional career. How could I ask what it was like to face life without a leg after renewing old memories about our simple trip?

OFTEN WE WERE IGNORED

My sixth victory in a row to open the season with Appleton in 1964 was almost finished and possibly, my fourteenth strikeout. I pushed off the mound a little harder, stretching my left leg a little further than normal. There was a flash of pain and I was on the ground unable to move. All the muscles in my lower back had been torn by the effort and, at this moment, I was paralyzed. What followed should provide a feeling as to the disregard for players and their well being during this era.

There were so many stock responses to injuries by the "good old boys" coaching, it was ridiculous. Their favorite was, "Rub some dirt on it". This could come after a player had been hit by a pitch or having broken his leg sliding, it didn't matter. There were no trainers at the lower levels and we had to administer to each other. No park below the AAA level had an ambulance available and most were far away from medical facilities.

Mike Andrews' compound leg fracture during our game in Waterloo, Iowa was the worst injury I would ever see during my career. Waterloo gained a lot of negative press during the 1963 season due to a brawl when players went into the stands battling their fans and our club was next to play in their stadium. Andrews was on the ground for twenty minutes when his spikes locked into a rotted first base bag. Another fight ensued when some drunk yelled "Throw a sheet over him, he's dead". Finally, an ambulance arrived and we continued the game.

Instead of being taken to the nearest hospital in Dubuque, my manager instructed teammates to carry me to the team bus, telling everyone to hurry their showers. The pain had lessened but there was a ten-hour ride ahead with all the terrible thoughts about whether my career was over.

We arrived at the park in Appleton and now I had to get to our apartment in the center of the city.

My two roommates, Steve Huntz and Eddie Hawkins, carried me in a locked, seated position from the bus to my car since the injured muscles had tightened during the night. I could operate the pedals but once at the apartment they had to extract and carry me to my bed on the second floor. Within minutes, I called out for help since nothing was going to get better lying there for any period of time.

Given the popularity of baseball in Appleton, word spread quickly in the hospital on my arrival and I was afforded VIP attention. Someone from staff called the front office demanding a representative be at the hospital because of the serious nature of my injury. My manager, Billy Demars, arrived as I was being taken to x-ray. Now he became concerned and, with permission from my doctor, placed a call to Baltimore while I was lying on my side, unable to straighten.

Baltimore was awaiting the diagnosis when Billy shouted, "What the hell is that"? The doctor had posted x-rays on the display board and the one person who shouldn't have been in the room was offering his diagnosis before the professional. Hearing this exclamation, I knew I was done not only professionally but also personally, never to walk again.

"Calm down, this indicates his bones are still growing. There are no skeletal problems, it is muscular". Demars passed this diagnosis to whomever was on the other end of the line with a false sincerity of concern. Twelve hours earlier he could have cared less. Rub some dirt on it. For the first time I was able to relax both body and mind.

Appleton's hospital was booked solid and the only room available was in a psychiatric wing. Nights proved to be interesting since nurses on duty tended to congregate in my room for relief. Once the traction device straightened my body and the morphine injections stopped, it was an ideal setting for someone famous. There were two weeks of intense therapy and I was ready to leave after a date with one particular nurse had been confirmed.

Ultra sound located the initial six major trouble spots and my therapist marked these with an X, using a ballpoint pen. A nurse armed with a large needle loaded with a muscle relaxant stabbed me at each indicated spot. If I didn't react by jumping off the table, she would stab again. Electric stimulation was soothing until the person running the machine increased amplification. My favorite therapy was the whirlpool and late night back rubs were a bonus. I was repaired and continued on to the 14-2 record, including our playoff game.

Pressures building from the war in Viet Nam caused me to make a decision at season end. While many college students were considering going to Canada, mine was whether I could afford time away from the game. I wasn't afraid of fighting and since I felt strongly about commitment, the only obstacle was the long interruption to my career if I were to be drafted.

Most players joined a Reserve program of the various services. There would be eight weeks of basic training followed by regular monthly meetings in their community. During each summer of obligation, their unit would go to a major base for two weeks of training. This is the route I chose.

Basic training was held at Ft. Jackson, SC requiring a long bus trip from Appleton. Our group of forty arrived at two am and gathered in front of barracks that were to be our temporary home. Diversity in our small population was amazing. Long hair, short hair, no hair, black, white, oriental, hippy garb and even a sport coat. The unknown aspect of our future caused a bonding at the bus station and increased during the trip. The next person to join us was downright scary because he was lean, mean, and in total control of our lives.

"Alright you sons of bitches, get off your ass and try to come up with some kind of formation. I doubt you're smart enough to understand my simple request, but we'll see. You're all mine from here on and I own your souls"! Never had I heard words delivered like these and could only wonder how much worse it could get.

"This is your last chance to get rid of any pornographic materials, drugs or drug paraphernalia. While I'm your babysitter, none of this shit is going to happen". Everyone was waiting for the first to make a move, but there wasn't a twitch. Not until I realized the bottom of my duffel bag held a shaving kit and in that kit was a hypodermic needle. The friendly nurses at the hospital wanted to give me a memento of my stay.

Now I had to upend this bag in front of everyone to find the kit and deliver the needle to my sergeant. Given the time of night, it was obvious this was something he didn't anticipate or want to deal with. But, true to his word, there were no questions asked. He now owned this junkie's soul for the next two months.

SHOWING OFF

One of my best ego boosters occurred during a two week Army Reserve training session at Ft. Leonard Wood, Missouri. This came mid summer during the 1967 season and my first year above the A classification. I was dominating everyone in the Eastern League and hated to sacrifice two weeks away. There was no preparation for the five am rousting by an unknown lieutenant since normal call for wakeup was six.

"Get up and get dressed, General Parish wants to meet you, there's a jeep waiting outside". Since there was to be no showering, I put on fatigues and off we went. When my driver passed beyond the base perimeter and not a word had been exchanged, I began to worry.

We arrived in a remote training area with a group of officers standing about. A colonel moved away returning with the general in tow. The commanding officer's expression changed dramatically the closer he got to this skinny kid from Norwalk. He had been told there was a professional pitcher under his command and he certainly didn't see that in me.

"Son, is it true you play professional baseball"? I spent the next fifteen minutes convincing him I was the real deal, short of being asked to throw a rock from the field we were standing in to show my arm strength. "We've got a game this weekend and I'm counting on you, do you understand"? I didn't understand but nodded my head in agreement in order to achieve a strategic retreat from this position. I had become a very important pawn in his personal chess game.

Because of the Reserve structure, every summer, professionals like me rotated through camp at various times. There were Army "bird dog" scouts similar to those in baseball. The difference was their assignment to find talent for the pleasure of top Army command at Leonard Wood. Once identified, we were forced to perform under any circumstances. You couldn't say no, you just hoped to survive without injury. Every organization looked the other way because of special favors granted in Reserve placements.

There were large amounts of money bet blindly on games by officers based only on limited advance information. This lack of proper intelligence has played out with far greater consequences in decisions other than baseball games. I don't know what would have happened to me if I had failed.

While warming up I had a flashback to my first game for Ohio University. Our freshman club had been "invited" to play Ohio State and their arrogance was evident when we stepped off the bus. The meeting was a double header and I had been given the status position as starter for the second game. This is a person who can save the day in case the first game is lost. As was expected by Ohio State, they embarrassed us winning by a large margin and now it was my turn.

After taking my initial warm up tosses, the entire Ohio State team came to the front steps of their dugout in order to offer insults. My build and appearance caused remarks never before delivered with as much sarcastic venom. Someone offered, "If you drank tomato juice, you'd look like a thermometer"! This was the most creative and others were insulting and crude. Their coach loudly ordered his entire bench to shut up and sit down when I struck out the side. We won easily and I accepted the coach's apologies for his team's behavior after the game.

There was no jeep ride to the park since I had failed initial inspection by the general during our brief field encounter. I only knew the time of the game and could only hope there would be a glove and spikes available.

Unfortunately the general didn't consider this to be important. I was relegated to pitching in my sneakers using a first baseman's glove found in the locker room.

The key to my performance would be the quality of the catcher and I had a good one. We were in sync from the first pitch and there was a feeling we had played together for several seasons. His physical makeup and game calling skills reminded me of someone I would face two years later in Carlton Fisk, but there was a huge difference. My catcher was twenty-three years old with five kids. He started his family at age fifteen in Kentucky and joined the Army as a last resort for a career. Few realize how many players in America have similar stories and never have a chance to show their abilities.

Time has dulled my memory as to the score but we won by a large margin. The general's smile and swagger increased each inning as he moved about the small stands. I was in total command of my battlefield and he knew it. The invitation to the Officer's Club after the game was a lot of fun since I was the only enlisted person there. The guy with the star on his lapels took care of any problem this might have presented. I left the club with an almost illegible note written by the general on a cocktail napkin excusing me from all duties for the rest of my stay. I placed this in the waste can outside the front door on my way back to the barracks.

The most surprising thing about the game for me was I hit a home run and this would be the only home run I hit in any park during my eight years as a pro, except if you count the one I hit off Cal Ripken Sr. in batting practice.

Rip was a manager who believed pitchers could have an impact during the year by improving their hitting. Normally, if you were a starting pitcher there was only an opportunity every five days to take a few swings during batting practice. A reliever never saw live pitching until he was facing pressures deep into a game. Rip dedicated himself during the

1965 season in Tri-Cities to throw batting practice to any pitcher who showed up one hour before regulars.

This was the only year Cal went beyond the norm for a manager except for when he drove the team bus in some league prior. We were even allowed to place a bat order with the Louisville Slugger bat company several times during the season with a choice of model and our name burned into the barrel. I found my last remaining S-2 (created by Stan Musial), 35 inch, 32-ounce Sommer model buried deep in a closet after my mom passed.

Most pitchers in professional baseball were stars at the high school level and believe they could play any position if given the opportunity. Sometimes a conversion at the professional level from an everyday player does happen and the reason is inability to hit a pitch that bends. My friend, Skip Lockwood, is a prime example. The scout who tabbed him as a "can't miss" third baseman saw Skip play only day games. When Lockwood couldn't pick up the rotation of a curve ball under night lighting it became evident a mistake had been made, but the bonus dollars were his to keep.

I was third in this day's early batting practice and every pitcher had come to enjoy one hour of Rip's time. Cal was younger than both Billy Harris and Steve Dalkowski and only seven years senior to me. To all of us, he seemed much older because of his commanding persona. Whenever we had an off day and my phone rang, I never turned down his request to baby-sit his children so he could take Vi out to dinner.

Having been a catcher, Rip's motion and speed were precise every time he delivered a pitch. The velocity was about seventy five per cent of an average professional pitcher, but his control was phenomenal and seldom anything was delivered above the belt to hit. Occasionally, just to mess with our minds, he would bend the ball without notice making everyone look foolish. He had as much fun as we did. But we were seeing pitches on a regular basis and it did provide a winning edge several times during the season.

On my second swing I hit a ball that produced a strange sensation. There was no feeling of impact to send a message to the hands. This only occurs when ball meets the bat in a very narrow zone and dependent on several factors. I didn't feel a thing and watched something of beauty. For the first time in my career, a ball left the park in fair territory. I couldn't wait for the next pitch but there would be none since Rip had thrown his glove down on the mound with mock disgust. "I quit. Anytime Sommer takes me deep it's time to pack it in"!

Everyone watched as he walked to the clubhouse expecting his return, but there wasn't to be one. Some who had come early to take swings were upset with my newly found power. But we all knew it was an act and part of the great atmosphere, energy and team chemistry he produced for all of us. If this blast had happened during a regular game, I would have stood at home plate to watch.

To me, the reward for Ripken's devotion to his pitchers came during a game where I was locked up in a duel with Chuck Dobson. We were the two best for each club and since Chuck went on to a major league record of 74-69 but only hit .153, my success this night had to really irritate him. It would be the only multi-hit game of my career and I had three of them this night. Dobson's catcher was Dave Duncan and for whatever reason, Dave and I had become friends carrying over to the following season.

The first hit came on a carom off home plate arcing so high the third baseman had no chance to throw me out. The second was a check swing and a bloop over second base. On the first pitch of my third at bat, with the winning run in scoring position, Duncan declared, "Let's see you hit this".

Chuck threw a nasty slider over the outside part of the plate but I was swinging wildly at anything and contact produced a line drive almost beheading Dobson. A few steps out of the box I heard swearing from Dave similar to that prior to a game on our last road trip.

The old park at Modesto had the visitor's route to the field passing by the left entrance to their clubhouse. Our manager, Harry Malmberg, was twenty feet ahead of me but I was able to hear the question from Duncan since his locker had a view out the door. "Skipper, who's going tonight"? "Sommer". Within the few seconds for me to move forward, there was a scene that said everything in relation to dominance over a player.

When I glanced to the right I saw Dave jumping up and down on his catcher's mitt declaring, "Another goddamn 0-4 night"! I could have told this person what was coming but he couldn't have hit it. This carried forward to the following season in the California League when he hit 46 home runs, but not one off me. Duncan has become one of the best pitching coaches in the history of baseball and, in my opinion, has a chance for the Hall of Fame. The only smear to his career is he couldn't hit me a lick.

The Lewiston Broncs fielded a team this year with sixteen players having an opportunity to play at a higher classification sometime during the season. Twelve eventually reached the majors, all with the parent club, no trading involved. Seven went on to star status and long careers

We beat Lewiston for the pennant and I was winner and MVP of our final playoff game. Their players moved upward and we lay dormant since every Oriole club was winning due to the skills of the scouting department and the strength of the youthful front office led by Harry Dalton. The following spring I attempted to buy my contract from a shocked Lou Gorman.

Every year players are signed for bonus money and the "can't miss" label. Which pan out achieving this expectation is impossible to identify. If you were betting, odds would be better in Vegas. Many of the highly touted phenoms become what are known as, five o'clock hitters. Batting practice is spectacular, but come game time, they can't perform.

We had the opportunity to play against Reggie Jackson in his first professional games at his home park of Modesto, California. He had signed for $125,000 of Charley Finley's money coming out of Arizona State. There always is curiosity about big bonus babies and everyone watches these players carefully during batting and infield practice. Reggie didn't look much different than anyone else. He was tall, ran well, made contact with the ball and had a very strong arm from the outfield. There was nothing to separate him from the majority of players on both sides.

Jackson's first game against us proved to be an indicator of great things to come. He hit a home run off our pitching setting up what would be one of the funniest incidents in my eight-year career. The following day I was the starting pitcher and minutes before the game our manager, Harry Malmberg called a private meeting with me and my catcher, Cliff Matthew. This was surprising, as I couldn't recall Harry ever calling a meeting for any reason. He was quiet, mild mannered and always seemed as if he wanted to be doing something else with his life. Maybe it was because our team was so bad and nothing he attempted seemed to work.

"I don't know who this character Jackson is, but he isn't going to hit a home run against us tonight." Malmberg was agitated and followed with, "If he gets up with no one on, you're to drill him. That'll show him we do things differently here and he can't get away with the kind of shit he did in college."

I was shocked because this directive went against the code of ethics in professional baseball. Whatever happened yesterday was history and today was a new ball game. If retaliation was to be made, it should have been ordered the night before. This was my fourth season and considering myself to be a veteran, what was being ordered went against all I had been taught. I offered, "Harry, I don't think that's right. He hit the homer off our pitching last night. I didn't have anything to do with that." If anything, I never was one to back off an opinion without a believable explanation.

"I don't give a shit. If you don't hit him it's going to cost you $100 out of your paycheck"! This was alarming because this year I was making $750 a month and only for the months we actually played. I quickly had to figure a way out of this without Harry knowing. I grabbed Matthew aside and we had a meeting of our own. Cliff was one of the nicest guys I ever met and he would do just about anything for you. Minutes before the start of the game we came up with a plan.

"When this guy Jackson gets up and I've got to do what Harry wants, let him know what the deal is. I don't know if he'll go along with this but we have to give it a try because I can't afford to waste $100 on something this stupid." Matthew nodded his head but secretly I knew he was hoping there would be runners on and everything would be nullified. Of course, this was the viewpoint of a catcher caught in the middle. From my perspective, I didn't want to see any base runners for the entire game.

As it would happen, I retired the side the first inning setting up the exact scenario Malmberg wanted. I walked slowly to the mound to start the second wondering if our plan would work. I was going to attempt hitting Jackson with a mediocre fastball somewhere where it would hurt the least, his butt. In a short period of time there had to be a lot of coordination to pull this off. I took my warm ups and Reggie stepped in.

Cliff wasn't giving any signals but I could see his lips moving behind his mask. He was talking to Jackson and Reggie was listening. The more he talked I could see the umpire was now getting in on this and had bent over almost like he was about to call a pitch. As time dragged on, it appeared to fans in the stands that a strategic battle was taking place. A power hitter was facing a cowardly pitcher seemingly afraid to take any signal from his catcher.

Finally, Cliff nodded his head. No signal, just a nod. The plan was in place and Reggie had agreed to take the dive. I went into my windup and everything looked good. But, as I got close to my release point, he panicked and started to bailout. The only thing I could do was adjust to his movement trying to throw the ball to a point where he might end up. Reggie kept bailing and when I finally did hit him in the butt with a medium speed fastball, he was fully three feet out of the box and the fun began.

Jackson jumped to his feet and charged the mound. Hot on his heels was Matthew followed closely by our umpire. What the people in the stands, and most importantly Malmberg, couldn't see was everyone was laughing. I immediately knew I was safe and decided to make this a moment to remember. Normally in a situation like this, I would be in reverse heading for the outfield and looking for help from any corner. But this time I was the bravest guy on the field.

All arrived at a spot in front of the pitcher's mound with the umpire standing ten feet away laughing so hard there were tears. I decided to add realism to our brawl and took a fake punch at Reggie who had me in a bear hug. Jackson stood up and shook me like a rag doll, all the time laughing. Players from both teams now surrounded us but everyone had frozen because nothing they saw made sense. How could there be a baseball fight with everyone having a good time?

The final act took place in the dugout when everyone heard Malmberg yell, "Take that you son of a bitch, this is what pro ball is all about"! We had done it. Harry was happy; I saved $100 while developing a short-lived reputation as a scrapper and Reggie wasn't hurt. The next batter hit into a double play. No harm, no foul.

IT WAS HARD TO SURVIVE

Few people realize how little money came the way of minor league players during this era. Even though a minimum salary of $500 per month was in place, the cash didn't flow until season start and ended the last day. When checks stopped everyone had to scramble to survive until the following spring. It was a matter of pride to brag about what unusual occupation had been found. The best had to have been that of John Sepich. John was fair skinned and our minor league trainer, Jack Baker, invented a secret potion to cover Sepich each day. I remember walking into the training room earlier than normal to find Jack mixing, like a mad scientist in the movies, the last ingredient drop by drop.

The unusual nature of Sepich's job was he worked in a mushroom mine in Pennsylvania. This meant John never saw the light of day for an entire winter except for weekends. Apparently, played out coal mines are ideal for this type of agriculture. The temperature is constant all year long, humidity can easily be controlled and most importantly, it is always dark. This was why Baker's invention had to work for the person having the nickname of "Casper".

Everyone with a pre season contract below the AAA level in 1966 received a letter saying training camp was to be in Fernandina Beach, Florida. It wasn't until reporting was it known we were on our own to eat. Someone in the accounting office figured out we could live on $5 a day and $35 was handed out each Monday.

Every year we were challenged to find start up money since everyone went into hock during spring training and needed advances in order to survive. There were deposits for utilities, first month rent and the need to eat on a daily basis. This translated into at least a month for repayments to the front office to balance our accounts. A typical full season was only five months and the mortality rate on married player's careers was high because of the pressures.

Because every full season started and stopped at basically the same time, no player ever met any state's requirement for twenty-six weeks of continuous employment thus no chance of filing unemployment claim. That is, not until the 1967 season in Elmira and I chose to challenge the system.

We won the second half of our split season on the final day by beating Williamsport. I was the hero but easily could have been the goat. There was a one run lead in the ninth inning when I came in with a runner on third and two outs. After bouncing a curve two feet in front of home plate and over Johnny Burrow's shoulder, the action happened so fast it was hard to absorb.

John raced back to the screen and his return throw wasn't more than six inches off the ground. I started toward home at the same time as the runner with the slight advantage of distance, but this person outweighed me by fifty pounds. His footsteps were getting louder as I got into position over the plate.

I applied a tag directly facing the umpire making eye contact for a brief moment. Up went his right arm. The game was over and we were to play Binghamton in a three game playoff for the championship. Weather came into play from the beginning and there were several rain outs, extending the contractual obligation by Baltimore. We would lose the pennant but qualify for unemployment by one day under the six month or 180 day rule. My filing was made after returning to California.

It took a few weeks for approval and checks started arriving for the maximum $125 weekly benefit. This provided a means to almost pay for my apartment and eat. Then the letter arrived with the New York State seal printed on bonded paper and a watermark adding more weight to the message.

"We regret to inform you an error has been made in the approval of your claim. Benefits will cease immediately but if you wish to appeal this action, you may do so within thirty days of this notice. Previously paid monies will not have to be reimbursed to the State because there was no false reporting on your part, only faulty interpretation of benefit law by a State employee". I had just finished the best year of my career and now faced the prospect of welfare in order to survive.

The attachment to the letter sited the clause within every professional baseball contract stating one must receive written approval to participate in another professional sport during the off season. Thus, a binding agreement existed between the two entities. Technically you were not unemployed even though there were no payments made by the parent club for the seven-month separation.

In the history of baseball there have been less than a dozen players who were able to combine dual careers in professional sports. Probably the five most famous are Gene Conley, Steve Hamilton and Dave Debusschere who had the size and talent for the NBA and Deon Sanders and Bo Jackson in the NFL. By now I had beefed up to 150 pounds but no professional sport appealed to me other than bowling.

My first call for help was to the Major League Player's Association requesting monetary assistance to fight the system. I would need legal representation and I could hardly afford my phone bill for the calls, let alone a lawyer. After seven straight days of follow up, the answer was no. The unstated message was I had not risen to the level of importance to be considered for help. The second request went to a prominent Elmira law firm whose members loved to be seen rubbing elbows with players, but the answer was the same. In other words, we aren't going to take one penny out of our pot to help someone not having that all important bubble gum card. My argument about how important it was to provide support, possibly stopping someone from quitting, fell on deaf ears.

I filed an appeal and set about to do research on precedence in other states with the best attack coming from the state of California where I was living. There were hundreds of cases involving actors and actresses who were not contract players to a studio and receiving a regular salary. There would be brief periods of pay and long periods of trying to survive. Because of the movie industry's importance to California, all were allowed to collect unemployment benefits while awaiting stardom. There couldn't be a better fit for my case. I was prepared with court documents and newspaper clippings when I sat in front of the State's hearing representative.

The meeting was over in fifteen minutes without anything offered by the State other than, "Thank you for coming. Your case will be reviewed and a determination will be forwarded in the mail". Fortunately I was able to find a job working for Shell Chemical and didn't need New York's benefits, at least not at this point in my life. My presentation had been impressive even without a lawyer and I knew there was a potential win to help others.

"We are sorry to inform you the appeal made while residing in the State of California has been denied. New York State recognizes nationally there are many possible legal precedents but we feel none cover our decision better than a case decided by the courts of Oregon involving a collective group of fisherman".

The one page document cited a ruling from ten years prior where the fishermen had signed a contract under duress from a large cannery. They filed for unemployment when waters got rough and they couldn't go out to sea to earn a living to support their families and there were no monies coming to them even though they were under contract for a year. What the State of New York didn't provide was the legal appeal made to a higher Oregon court and the reversal of the lower court's decision.

Two years after my denial, someone with money won in court and all players were then able to collect benefits if they met the requirements. I gave it my best but didn't have two nickels in my jeans to rub together at the time.

A DIFFERENT ROUTE TO THE TOP

There are people in professional sports that arrive at the top, but not necessarily on the playing field. Few leave trails as to how they got there but there is one I am proud of, Herman Schneider of the Chicago White Sox. The same White Sox who brought home a World Series to the city in 2005 after 88 years of frustration, erasing the memory of the controversial 1919 "Black Sox" scandal where some players were accused of taking money to throw the Series.

Herm was our clubhouse attendant during the 1969 season in Rochester and one of the most liked persons involved with our club. At this point he was a high school junior who had the drive to succeed. He and his neighborhood friends would concoct ways of sneaking in Silver Stadium, getting caught more often than not. Eventually, Red Wing officials became so tired of reprimanding him they offered Herm a job.

Schneider did it all. He swept clubhouse floors, polished spikes, picked up dirty towels, washed uniforms and taped ankles. But the thing that intrigued him most was the trainer's job. I never had an injury this year, but whenever I needed Herm for something I knew where to find him. Many on our club over tipped him because of his enthusiasm and spirit. Mary and I provided rides whenever needed since his mother worked several jobs as a single mom.

I was watching the NBC Game of the Week one Saturday afternoon in 1979 and the White Sox were playing the Yankees. A line drive hit the Sox pitcher squarely on his shinbone and the announcer offered, "Here comes Chicago's trainer, Herm Schneider, to see how bad this is". The camera zoomed in and there was our ever-smiling clubhouse gofer on national television one decade removed from Rochester.

After graduating from Franklin High School, Schneider took sports medicine courses at Monroe Community College and spent the 1970 season as the Wings' assistant trainer. From there he landed a job in the Yankees organization and was an assistant trainer of the Yankee's teams that won the World Series in '77 and '78. He was there for Reggie Jackson's three home runs in a World Series game and Bucky Dent's homer against the Red Sox. Many thought he was crazy to leave New York to take the White Sox job in 1979, but Herm was eager to run his own program.

No one appreciated the job he did with the Sox more than their pennant winning manager, Ozzie Guillen. Herm helped him come back from a devastating knee injury when Guillen was a White Sox shortstop in the early 1990's. Schneiders's work with Guillen and slugger Bo Jackson earned him accolades from the sports medicine community and beyond.

It is ironic the Sports Illustrated edition of "Where are they now?" had Bo Jackson on the cover and a feature piece on Dalkowski in the same edition. Herm was given major ink about helping Jackson to recover from his hip replacement. It's no coincidence that when Michael Jordan decided to switch to baseball, he chose Schneider as his personal trainer.

After seeing Herm on television in 1979, I penned a heart felt congratulatory letter on his reaching the major leagues. His achievement was just as important to me as any player I knew. What came to mind was the smile on his face in the Rochester clubhouse when I gave him the sweater we bought because Mary and I liked him. Recently I mailed my Association of Professional Ball Players of America ballot (I'm life member #3322) voting for Herm to be on their Board of Directors. We were allowed to vote for ten and he was my number one pick.

82

MY EXPOSURE TO HOLLYWOOD

I doubt anyone from my Norwalk, Ohio graduating class ever had lunch with a bona fide Hollywood blond sex symbol, but I did. My purchase of a 1963 Playboy came to life in Lodi, California three years later when I broke bread with Mamie Van Doren and her husband, Lee Meyer, in their apartment.

Mamie had posed twice in Playboy to promote her movie, "Three Nuts in Search of a Bolt" with the character name of "Saxie Symbol". Lee and I had competed against each other for three straight years and had become good friends. My invitation to dine with the couple came one afternoon after running into Meyer while shopping in Stockton.

My favorite men's store was located near the University of Pacific campus. It was upscale and pricey, but I would visit every other week looking for the largest markdowns I could afford. Across the street was a record shop that was jammed all afternoon with college students, meaning a lot of girls were there. In this era, there were listening booths where vinyl records could be played before buying but the main attraction was young people being together.

Early afternoon I entered John Fall Men's Store to look for bargains and saw Lee sorting through racks at the rear. He was so intent; my approach wasn't noticed until I was almost standing next to him. When we did make eye contact there was an immediate flush to his face and I could see why. He was going through a display of satin underwear of various colors. This was very radical for the time, even for California.

"What's going on"? Lee's color returned to normal and he answered, "Oh man, Mamie's done with summer stock in

LA and she's coming up here for a couple of months. She likes this shit and I've got to buy a supply. I'm not even going to try them on because I know they'll feel creepy. I can't let anyone know about this. You won't tell anyone on your club will you"? After assuring Lee his secret would go to the grave with me, we settled into normal banter. But I think his guilt built to a point when he made an amazing offer. "Do you want to come over to the apartment some day for lunch and meet Mamie"?

Mamie was born, Joan Lucille Olander, in Rowena, South Dakota, February 6, 1931. Her mother named her after Joan Crawford. After the family moved to Los Angeles, Joan went to work as an usherette at the Pantages Theatre in Hollywood in 1946. In the summer of 1949 she won the titles, "Miss Eight Ball and "Miss Palm Springs". While doing the Miss Palm Springs contest she was discovered by Howard Hughes. She lunched with him and he gave her a bit part in "Jet Pilot" at RKO, which was a movie starring John Wayne in 1957. Her line of dialog consisted of one word, "Look!"

She later signed a contract with Universal. The studio had big plans for her, hoping she would bring the success that 20th Century Fox had with Marilyn Monroe, the reigning sex symbol of the era. It has been said that because the day she was signed was also the day President Eisenhower was inaugurated, the studio decided to give her the name Mamie for Ike's wife and Van Doren because it sounded Dutch.

While she and the other blond bombshells did not attain the same level of superstar status as Monroe, Van Doren did become one of the leading sex symbols of the day. Marilyn, Mamie and Jane Mansfield were known as the "Three M's," and Van Doren achieved legendary status as the sole survivor. But while Monroe did "Gentlemen Prefer Blondes" and Mansfield had a big success with "Will Success Spoil Rock Hunter?" Universal stuck Van Doren with Francis the talking mule and "Francis Joins the WACS".

Mamie had five husbands and Meyer was number three, lasting two years. In her tell all autobiography, "Playing the Field", she acknowledged numerous affairs, including ones with Clark Gable and Joe Namath. She also had an on again, off again, engagement with Bo Belinsky and I believe it was Bo who did the introduction to Lee.

The day of our luncheon date I woke up as nervous as I had been for my first professional start in baseball. Their apartment was easy to find in Lodi and typical for what a poorly paid minor league player could afford. How could a Hollywood star be staying in what could be classified as a "dump" after having been discovered by Howard Hughes? It took a while before I was able to leave my car and ring the doorbell.

Lee greeted me with, "Hi Slim, come on in. Mamie's in the bedroom and she'll be right out". In the bedroom? Was she going to appear in some slinky silk negligee in order to make an impression and perpetuate the sex symbol image? When she walked into the living room I was stunned.

Walking toward me, with a welcoming hand outstretched and a beautiful smile, was a person who had the looks of a co-ed on the University of Pacific campus in Stockton. Her hair was shorter than publicity photos of the day and she was wearing a cashmere sweater with tailored silk pants that must have come from Rodeo Drive in Hollywood. "Hi, I'm Mamie. I'm glad to meet any friend of Lee's. I've put together a little lunch if you're ready to eat".

After the initial shock of sitting down to dine with a legend wore off, the conversation moved on to broad ranging subjects, none of which were about our respective professions. It was amazing as to how intelligent Mamie turned out to be and we left Lee in the dust for the next hour. When it became time to leave, she walked me to the door and gave me a polite kiss on the cheek. It is absolutely amazing I didn't miss Stockton on the return to my apartment and land in Sacramento.

Our next playing date with Lodi was three weeks later and their club had latched onto a rare promotion event for the minor leagues. "Meet Mamie and Lee". The winning entrant would have the chance to duplicate my luncheon experience but not in the same environment I enjoyed. There were entry blanks not only at the park but also all over town.

The response was greater than what management anticipated and the night of the event found so many people coming through the gates, they had to rope off both the left and right field lines for standing room only. Fortunately, I wasn't our starting pitcher this night and could sit back and enjoy the drama.

Once everyone settled in, including those standing ten deep along the lines, a lengthy introduction began by the announcer in the press box. Upon concluding, Mamie appeared along with Lee walking up to home plate where the field microphone had been set up. I wasn't prepared for the image change, even though I knew she was a star.

Mamie was dressed in a form fitting, silver lame', micro mini skirt with high heels that were having a hard time providing support since they were digging into the grass on the way to home plate. She was in her prime at thirty-five and nothing had impacted her looks or figure. Because of the unevenness of her step, everything was in motion and jiggling, much to everyone's delight. This is what a star is all about. Her "Glad to be here in Lodi and seeing all you wonderful fans" speech was short and it was time to draw the winning entry.

Since the entry barrel was so large, a platform had been provided in order for Mamie to pull the winning entry. She and Lee climbed the three steps and after the barrel had rotated sufficiently, it was time for the drawing. The hatch was opened but she had to lean over to a great degree in order to reach into the center of the drum to select a winner. Now is when the home team dugout came into play.

While Mamie was bent over and rummaging for a ticket, Lee happened to turn around to look at his teammates. They were bunched in a tight group and because of the viewing angle, all were able to enjoy the rear view of this sex symbol leaning over the barrel. In one of the best showmanship moves I have ever seen, Lee removed his ball cap with an exaggerated slowness and placed it below his wife's skirt. Five thousand fans and fifty players erupted with both laughter and applause and I could feel her soft kiss on my cheek leaving her apartment.

PIT STOPS ON THE ROAD

Every year the anticipation of going to spring training was exciting for many reasons. Most obvious would be chasing the dream, but it can be broken down further. The physical and emotional clocks had been reset and age could be ignored for the moment.

Always it was a wonderful opportunity to experience the size and diversity of America while traveling from spring training to whatever destination had been assigned. Once on the road, there were opportunities to absorb many flavors of life along the way. Life experiences provided the tempering required for survival as a professional. Tempering of hot metal imparts a hard exterior with a flexible interior allowing steel to bend without breaking. This is what is required of a professional athlete.

During daylight hours I tried to take a large chunk out of my distance, along with the vow I wouldn't drive past sunset. I would get to my destination on my own terms and suffer the consequences for being late. Never would there be a motel room in a major city, always finding the smallest town with character close by. This was possible since Interstate travel was incomplete and a decision had to be made prior to the sun lowering. Somewhere in Alabama I saw my life flash before my eyes when I heard a deep male voice yell, "Gun"!

My rules on the road were, always ask the desk clerks for their favorite spot to eat and where to go for entertainment not far from the motel. In a small town, they were usually the same and I set off to find the "roadhouse" recommended.

After dinner, I joined the locals at the bar and waited for the right spot to join in their conversations. The result was usually the same no matter where I was in the country. Once my slight fame was slipped into the mix, I couldn't buy a drink for the rest of the evening and could enjoy celebrity status. The secret was to listen carefully and decide when to give the verbal tap on the shoulder.

This night I violated one of my covenants. Never would I stray from home base in a territory completely foreign to me. I guess the promise of live music and beautiful women was too tempting when an invitation was offered to travel a "short piece" and have a great time. Since I didn't have to drive, it made sense to accept the local's offer without worrying about consequences.

I was comfortable until our driver made a left turn off the highway ten miles out of town and we were on a dirt road threading our way through tall pines for half a mile. The view was no different from the advanced infantry night training exercises at Ft. Polk, La. riding in a deuce and a half going deep into the swamps to play war games. There would be a major difference in comparisons soon since our exercises at Polk used blank bullets.

Everything my new friends had described was there as we pulled in. We had a hard time finding a place in the grass parking lot since it was prime time for everyone to arrive. One of our group sprinted ahead to secure a table while yelling out greetings to many of the women arriving in their own caravans. It couldn't get any better for the Ohio Yankee, in the heart of Dixie, looking for a good time.

This would be my first experience with what came to be known as "Southern Rock" and the band was dynamic. It was obvious they had a following in the middle of nowhere and since every famous band has to have a beginning, it is quite possible they might have been the Allman Brothers. Brothers Gregg and Duane had gone on the road after graduating from high school in Daytona Beach this year and were playing together for the first time as the "Allman Joys".

Years later when I heard their famous sound, it was the same as this night in Alabama.

My hosts had done an incredible job of gathering women to our table using a combination of local knowledge and my strange uniqueness. It was exciting since there was someone seated next to me listening to my every word, knowing this would be a one-night stand.

At the end of the evening the band started playing slow sets, which were perfect for couples making mating decisions for the night. My fun was ruined when somebody decided another was "messin" with his woman and pulled a weapon to make his point. Fortunately, we were on the other side of the dance floor and no one hesitated for a second in making the decision to leave via the screened window next to our table.

The first person to leave broke through the screening and we all followed in various ways. Having gone through military training the previous year, I dove headfirst and did a barrel roll easily catching up to the group heading for the car. We heard a gun shot as we left the parking lot but none of us said anything. This was way beyond the norm for my friends and I knew their minds were on what might have happened to someone they knew. For me, I was on the road the next day never to know.

Living history books are a rare find but I found one of the best outside Albuquerque on my way to play in the Northwest League in 1965. The bar next to the motel was the focal point and reason for being built first and not vice versa. Walking through the front door gave me the feeling I had entered a Hollywood movie set during the filming of any classic Western. Difference was, this setting dated back to the 1920's and everything was authentic, including the person who would spend the next four hours telling stories about his life that couldn't have been written better by any writer.

This personage could have been the famous "Marlboro Man" used in their advertising for years. Handsome, square jawed, weathered skin, wearing the most striking white Stetson I had ever seen. His boots were scuffed just enough and the Levi outfit was faded just right. I sat for more than thirty minutes without saying a word before attempting conversation. There was plenty of character around to absorb, including what appeared to be bullet holes in various places in the woodwork. I would learn over the course of the evening they were real and as locals became comfortable with me, their histories came out.

I couldn't wait any longer. "Do you know anything about this bar? I'm just traveling through and I've never seen anything like it. There's nothing in Norwalk, Ohio like this". To me, it was a perfect intro telling him I was from far away, interested in history, and since there was a fifty-year gap in our ages he could be my educator.

My friend was seventy-five years old and only in the last five years had slept on a mattress because of the inevitable pains caused by aging. His cowboy career started at age fifteen, seven years prior to both New Mexico and Arizona becoming states and his birth was only twenty-five years beyond the end of the Civil War. He opened up to me with the need to tell stories just like Lefty Grove, only there was far more time to enjoy.

It took a while before getting up nerve to ask, "Did you ever fight any indians"? The Battle of Little Big Horn where Custer made his famous "last stand" was just fourteen years removed from his birth date. The only indians familiar to me were those located in Cleveland and had become my enemy after signing with Baltimore.

"Early on in my cowboyin' we had trouble all the time since more and more land was being taken over by settlers from back east. The ranch owners I worked for just kept gettin' bigger though I don't know nothin' about how they got the land. The tribes kept splittin' up because they couldn't agree about what to do. Young ones wanted to fight but the old timers had given up. It wasn't long before all we had to worry about was rustlers. "Came close to hangin' one of those no good sons of bitches once. I still think we should have done it". He went on to paint a word picture providing me a front row seat to the action.

Wherever his herd was there was a terrible thunderstorm this day, creating havoc because of the lightning and thunder. It is a cowboy's worst nightmare in trying to maintain crowd control because it was inevitable groups would splinter and head off in all directions. This is a major part of the term, "roundup".

"I come up a rise by myself and there were five or six cows being herded down a wash and away from our main group by two guys I never seen before. In times like this you had to be careful it wasn't part of another drive that was havin' the same problem you were. But when one guy lit off and left his partner there alone, I drew my gun and pointed straight at this guy's head. I wasn't much of a shot, but he didn't know that. I brought him back to the rest of our bunch and we decided to have some fun".

"We could have killed him on the spot and he knew it. Hardly any cowboy had family and nobody could have found a hole dug out in the middle of nowhere. We found a tree nearby and looped a rope over a branch. Nothin' was said while were doing this, but his eyes said it all. He knew he was goin' to be a dead man soon, one way or the other. Somebody made a noose and we stared at him for a couple of minutes. Finally one of our guys rode up along side and whacked his horse in the rump sending them on their way. We knew this guy would never bother us again".

It wasn't until I saw the 1991 movie, "City Slickers" with Jack Palance as "Curly Washburn", would there be a reminder of this cowboy. Curly was a rugged seventy year plus ex-cowboy who held the key to finding lost gold somewhere in the West. Billy Crystal was part of a group of easterners out for a dude ranch experience who became involved in the plot. Palance won a Best Supporting Actor Oscar and during his acceptance speech, dropped to the floor and did a series of one-arm push-ups, which had been a classic move within the movie. I know my man could have done the same.

I TRIED TO ESCAPE FROM BONDAGE

Our lives are a collection of experiences and, as we age, memories are revisited often and a career changing moment is not hard to identify. The aging multiplier is severe in professional sports and any incident has a greater impact over a normal business career.

My mistake wasn't allowing the eye examiner to alter my records during an initial physical for the Army. He located me in the blood pressure line changing my records from 4F to1A. I could only read E on the chart without glasses but had become part of the herd mentality and didn't question his actions. Nor was it when my manager at Appleton, Billy Demars, canceled my opportunity to pitch against the major league club in an exhibition game in Aberdeen, South Dakota.

My record at the time was 7-0, leading the Midwest League in everything. Two starters developed sore arms and because Billy was more interested in his own self-promotion, he refused to allow my trip. I had been used the week before as a closer for the first time with great results. I struck out the side in the ninth inning on fourteen pitches feeling what an adrenaline rush can do to the body. Demars knew his pennant possibilities would be enhanced if I stayed to handle multiple duties. My substitute performed well, joining the Orioles as a starter the following season.

Spring training of 1966 had potential to be the most exciting camp of my short career but instead, became a pivotal point for the wrong reasons. My combined record for the two previous years was 26-9, including playoff games. The only reward was a championship ring handed out by the Northwest League commissioner after our win in 1965.

We knew this wouldn't be something encrusted with diamonds when he approached our team along the third base line. The rings were inside a cigar box and since all were the same size, it didn't matter which was picked. The interior portion of our award was painted black, overlapping the supposed gold on the outside.

Contract negotiations were historically conducted by mail resulting in every minor league player giving in. All wanted to play baseball but had no bargaining power. It may sound crazy in this age of average salaries nearing three million dollars per year, but no one ever discussed money as a motivating factor. There was amazement we were actually receiving money to do what we had done as little boys.

I became the first minor league player in Orioles' history coming unsigned to the minor league camp. I walked in demanding to negotiate face to face with someone. I can't remember what prompted this move, but it had to do with my viewpoint concerning common sense. Why couldn't I get the salary I wanted and if not, why couldn't I go elsewhere to play?

The person assigned to handle this renegade was Lou Gorman. Lou was a New Englander who seemed oddly out of sync from the norm of baseball executives at the time. Professional baseball was in the beginning of transformation much like that of a butterfly. The cocoon held larvae about to be born replacing moths that had been the backbone of baseball for almost eighty years. Lou was Harry Dalton's protégé and another future executive, John Schuerholtz, was conducting bed checks. Gorman went on to become Boston's General Manager and Scheurholtz Atlanta's.

Lou was a skilled wordsmith but I believe he met his match in me. The one hour meeting was going nowhere as we argued merits in my trying to achieve a $200 per month increase. Baseball contracts, at this time, did not bind major league teams to anything. If you were released one day into the season there was no obligation on the club's part to pay any remaining agreed upon money.

Lou's arguments were ridiculous as to why my reasonable request couldn't be met. It digressed to where Gorman quoted my times in the 60-yard dash. We were getting nowhere with logic and looking at each other with facial expressions showing our frustration. "Your times in the 60 aren't up to the average for the camp".

Deep within I remembered a classic story going back a few years. Cleveland's general manger had hired a world-class sprinter, Harrison Dillard, to teach running to all in spring training, including pitchers. The reaction from one veteran was, "If running was so god damn important to pitching, then Man of War (a famous race horse) would have been a 20 game winner"! Once I hit Lou with this response I didn't give him any time before the knockout punch.

"Lou, if my value to the Orioles is so minimal, the only solution is for Baltimore to sell me my contract for fair market value". Lou's face went blank and his canned team responses stopped. Gorman was always in the lead during negotiations, much like a master chess player. Many times his thinking was so far forward he couldn't absorb parts of the immediate conversation. Our feeling was, if asked about his recently deceased dog, Lou would answer, "Good, good, now what about your contract?" This was a common opinion amongst players resulting in the nickname of Lou "Good Good" Gorman, said with affection, not mocking.

My father had offered to advance several thousands of dollars to purchase my contract from the Orioles. This came after one of the few personal discussions about my wants and needs. I had to explain obstacles ahead and a certainty I could go nowhere else while I was under contract to Baltimore.

The bluff caused a turning point in the negotiations. "I have another meeting. Can we get together tomorrow at eleven?" To me, this sounded like a concession and validated my militant stance. I had no agent since there weren't many at this time in sports and I was on my own. My hotel room that night was the rear seat of my 1960 Corvair, falling asleep to the smell of fresh orange blossoms.

At the appointed hour, I entered the tiny office afforded Lou. His desk had a single yellow contract placed perfectly in the center. The previous day's papers that had been scattered were gone and the minimal approach had an impact. "Take a look at this". What I saw was exactly what I wanted. How could I be faulted for signing at that point?

Many years later I would learn the bravado had panicked Baltimore into believing I might be the hole in the dike allowing free agency waters to enter. Little did they know how few dollars I had in my war chest. It was to be several years later when free agency was born. It also must have been why Lou offered me the Kansas City minor league pitching coach position and the gm position with their Florida A club within a month after my retirement.

Curt Flood was as crucial to the economic right of ballplayers as Jackie Robinson was to breaking the color barrier. Flood was fully aware as to the social relevance of his rebellion against the baseball establishment. With the backing of the Players Association and with former U.S. Supreme Court Justice, Arthur Goldberg arguing on his behalf, Flood pursued the case known as, "Flood v. Kuhn (Commissioner Bowie Kuhn) from January 1970 to June 1972 at district, circuit, and Supreme court levels. Although the Supreme Court ultimately ruled against Flood, upholding baseball's exemption from antitrust statutes, the case set the stage for the 1975 Messersmith-McNally rulings and the advent of free agency. Baseball would never be the same again.

MY CAREER WAS OVER

It is difficult to describe the euphoria when realization of one's goal occurs in a professional sport. You are the best at your position and could throw the winning touchdown in the Super Bowl or strikeout the final batter to win the World Series. This matched perfectly with my childhood dreams.

Spring training in 1966 was moving forward nicely and what happened is still hard to comprehend, since each outing was better than the one before. To have a career influenced by one event is difficult to understand for those whose occupations cover decades of employment.

My final start of the camp in Fernandina produced a 5 inning, 7 strikeout, 0 run effort against the AA club managed by Darrell Johnson. Johnson had started managing within the Orioles organization at the AAA level in Rochester after a mediocre playing career. Somehow, he managed to get demoted to the AA level after the previous season. Cal Ripken sought me out to say I had officially made the Elmira club.

Little was known about Johnson, except for the reputation and rumors he was a Don Juan of major league status. His sexual conquests, purportedly, were recorded in a "black book". Supposedly, there had been offers to purchase this information over the years since it included several movie stars.

Johnson had been demoted after managing Rochester to three years of indifferent results, never challenging for a pennant. Someone in the organization placed him at the helm of the AAA club immediately after his playing days were over, assuming he knew how to handle players at this level. Unfortunately we crossed paths during the wrong time in my career.

Fernandina Beach, Florida only had two bars we knew of. One was near the center of the village and fairly respectable. The other was several miles away and could be hostile toward players since we were in competition for local females. Players and management had an agreement. Neither would invade each other's turf.

Howie Stethers and I ended this evening at our bar even though we really wanted to go where the action was. There is no logical way to explain how our careers and lives were about to be altered.

Howie was a veteran who had played in Elmira several seasons before. Despite being the rare left-handed commodity, he hadn't progressed as might be expected. We played together the previous season at Tri-Cities in the Northwest League and Stethers had proven to be a winner (10-4) playing for Cal Ripken. Rip was a manager who pushed for promotions for those who had helped him, just like Weaver.

Since we knew our placements it would be fun to join together sharing his local knowledge. Curfew was midnight but never was there enforcement and it would be difficult for management to make this an issue.

Any of us having spent a few years in the minor league camp had tales to tell about those in Baltimore's ivory towers. Most stories centered on out of control actions at the Elks Club by staff and came from locals. One of my favorites was that of a coach giving sliding demonstrations in the middle of a dance floor, concluding with a hook slide into the jukebox. These memories were before money changed the picture.

Curfew came and passed for Howie and me but we were in a mood not influenced by alcohol, just anticipation as to how well we were going to perform. A protective blanket is created during spring training for anyone who has excelled and survived. One more year is available to pursue your dream and new dogs biting at your heels have been put aside. Because of the effect of conditioning, everyone's mental attitude is as positive as it can be and expectations are for a perfect season. Nothing else enters the mind.

The front door opened and there stood the most beautiful girl either of us had seen in our six weeks of camp. Her eyes quickly surveyed the bar's interior. Howie and I were the class amongst the twenty patrons since we were dressed with something other than Levi's and T-shirts. Her beauty shocked us to the point we stopped talking and awaited her next move. She came directly to our table. "Can I join y'all"? Before I could think of a response, Howie coolly said, "Sure". What came next dictated our respective careers as our queen quickly described why she was in our bar and at our table.

Previously she had been in the coaches' bar but encountered a drunken staff member. This person had been physical and suggestive sexually to the point she fled afraid for her safety. Why she didn't go home didn't come into play in either Howie's mind or mine. As she finished her story, the door opened and the person she had just described entered. It was our manger, Darrell Johnson. The distance from door to our table was about twenty feet. Fear was obvious in our local since she could read our body language and facial expressions. Johnson went to the bar and ordered a beer.

The bartender was a person normally handling late night duties. This was a young man who knew simple mixed drinks but more importantly, had the size to handle a forced exit of anyone who went out of control. This was our bar, he knew us, and I assume he knew the young lady at our table. But he didn't know the drunk who could ruin this night for all of us.

Once Darrell had a beer he turned toward us leaning on the bar for stability trying to project an image of authority. Howie and I were mapping out where we were going to live, eat, and how to use the AA springboard to the majors. We were not prepared for this confrontation at all.

Johnson left the bar without drinking any beer and his exit was the same as his entrance except for hitting the wall just before the door. Our bartender had been braced for a fight and the young lady was expecting another advance from Johnson. Howie and I were anticipating a mild rebuke the following morning, but what happened was beyond comprehension.

Roster assignments were at 10am and 100 players were gathered. The daily ritual was to have a staff member announce rosters and this particular day the chore fell upon John Schuerholtz. John was in his first year of professional baseball, assigned duties such as conducting bed checks and arranging transportation home for those who didn't make it. Today, he is the president of the Atlanta Braves and one of the most respected persons in baseball.

John announced the Elmira roster and shock spread through our gathering since Howie and I were gone. Immediately Johnson made a declaration. "There was a violation of camp rules and conduct last night that can't be tolerated"! Sommer and Stethers are no longer on the Elmira team and because of this violation they will run fifty laps."

Howie and I looked at each other trying to understand what had happened and how to respond. I looked for Cal Ripken but he was nowhere in sight. Quickly I realized we were being sacrificed since Johnson couldn't have either of us around during the season armed with our previous night's knowledge.

Our fifty-lap punishment was across the width of three outfields used at the Fernandina Beach complex. The distance would be roughly three miles. Johnson added to the humility by stopping what little practicing was going on for everyone to feel his control.

We started on a routine trot, but after ten laps we realized what a physical effort it was going to be. The worst part was the humiliation in front of the players and our inability to confront this dictator. This was a hazing no one in the Baltimore family had ever seen.

Halfway through Howie stopped and threw up. "Screw Johnson, I quit!" While I briefly stopped to offer help, there was a realization my career was on the line if I didn't do as ordered. The further I went an anger built within. I had enough time to analyze how unjust this was and what my reaction was going to be.

I completed my fiftieth lap with the proverbial piano on my back and did a hook slide into our clubhouse door. Howie was on his hands and knees crawling to the clubhouse. At this point my mind was clear as to the next move. Slowly I drew erect and waited until I had the attention of everyone before offering a middle finger salute to Johnson.

With this release of emotion, I knew my career was over. Not because I was demoted, but because this violated my sense of fairness. It you work hard and succeed you will be rewarded. This was how I was raised and couldn't accept anything less.

As I was packing my gear, the biggest concern was how to explain to Grandmother Murphy why I was quitting. She was my biggest supporter about grabbing for the brass ring and in the early fifties owned one of the first televisions in her neighborhood. It was a Fada, whose name was derived from the brilliant electronics engineer, Frederic Anthony D'Andrea. During the 1950's, his television sets were widely held to be the absolute best available and grandma had one. When the Cleveland Indians were on, all activity in her house stopped.

Heading toward my car, I was intercepted by someone from management whom I had not seen during our degradation. George Bamberger looked at me and lifted his right hand like a traffic cop. My anger was intense but this silent signal caused me to pause.

George was our minor league pitching coach and had a very direct, no nonsense approach about pitching and, more importantly, how the game should be played. He was an important cog in the Orioles organizational wheel along with Cal Ripken, producing future championships. His dedication to and understanding of "The Oriole Way" allowed him to reach his zenith later as manager for Milwaukee.

Bamberger guided me away from our small clubhouse and far from players or staff. "Tim, I don't know how to explain what happened. All I can tell you is this son of a bitch will be gone next season. Suck it up and go have the best year you can have. Trust me, he'll be gone." What I didn't know was the pent up dislike for Johnson within the Oriole ranks. I firmly believe it was due to his going against the grain of team unity required by Dalton, Gorman, Weaver, Ripken, Bamberger and many loyal lieutenants extending to the "bird dog" level within the organization.

Immediately, a sense of order was established and I accepted the words of a person I trusted. "George, I'll go because of what you've said, but I can't understand why I'm being punished. My record speaks for itself and there is no one on that club who can match my last two years and what I've done this spring!"

Slowly, George shifted his focus from me and looked up at the oak tree we were underneath taking a deep breath. This veteran of eighteen years as an active player was trying to give me the sense of his own frustration. He was a player who only had the "cup of coffee" in the bigs despite his credentials in the minors. He had sacrificed his soul to the game. "You'll have a great year at Stockton and then everything will be wide open."

Because of this last minute change I didn't know many teammates because of their newness to the game. I was coming off a two year combined record of 26-9, MVP of a club, starting pitcher for an all-star game and now, totally in shock.

George's prediction came true the following year. Despite Johnson's club winning the Eastern League pennant by 20 games and a .637 percentage, he was gone from the organization and out of a managing job anywhere the next year. I have never been able to find out the circumstances for the firing, but it was obvious the glove didn't fit. Johnson migrated to the Red Sox organization and was fired the year after his team played in the 1975 World Series.

Momentum is a word often used to describe brief periods during any athletic contest, but seldom for an entire season. Only two Stockton players this year made the major leagues, while ten from Elmira advanced. Our club finished more than thirty games out of first place, and we didn't have any fun.

I led all Class A pitchers in innings pitched with 226 and a win-loss record of 11-17. My ERA of 2.87 was within the top 10 of the league. Of the 17 losses, I was beaten 13 times by one run. The most memorable of the one run losses was after losing for the fifth straight time. My manager declared I had no curfew while all others were to be in their rooms by midnight in Bakersfield. "Sommer, you can get drunk, laid, whatever you want to do. I don't want to see you until game time tomorrow."

His directions came as we pulled into the motel parking lot. My spirits had been lifted and I left our bus on a high. I soon realized we were three miles out of town; I had no transportation and little money in my pocket. It was a great psychological ploy used by my manager. Within the hour I was in someone's room playing nickel and dime poker.

There was a reason why I didn't reach the major leagues. Not because of physical problems or poor performances. It was a five-minute encounter with someone who had total control over my life at that time. Had I been able to bluff Lou Gorman into selling my contract, or free agency was available, things would have been different.

UNDERSTANDING WHAT IT TAKES

Professionals enjoy being in the company of athletes from other venues wishing they had similar skills. Their common bond is the drive required to reach the top of his or her sport. This relationship came home after playing in fifteen LPGA pro-am events at the Corning Classic in Corning, NY.

Every minor league player who played with or against Michael Jordan during Birmingham's 1994 season in the Southern League has a story to tell. To me, this was the ultimate crossover in all of sports history. The greatest basketball player of all time was attempting to reach the major leagues. Unfortunately, .a .202 average with 3 home runs just wasn't enough and he was gone.

Each pro-am was electric since I was going to be playing with someone possessing the same drive and willing to gamble a significant portion of their life chasing a dream. Lisa Depaulo showed the best example of this determination to me. Lisa was featured in a 2000 Sports Illustrated edition with a heading;

*MY SHOT-I'm finally making my LPGA debut
as a 34-year old rookie.*

The name of this column couldn't be more appropriate, because after 12 long years of trying to get on the LPGA tour, I'm finally getting my shot this season. When I tee it up for the first time in 2000 at this week's Cup Noodles Hawaiian Ladies Open, I'll be one of the oldest rookies on the tour. I began my quest back in 1987, when I first entered Q school as a 21 year old fresh out of the University of Texas. Now I'm 34 and a veteran of the Asian tour, the Futures tour and other mini-tours too numerous to mention. I've won seven times, but my average annual income over the last 11 years has been less than $20,000. I might have earned my card a decade ago except for a mental fumble that bothers me to this day. In 1989 I went to the final stage of Q school with my confidence at an all time high. I had won a Futures event the week before and was totally focused on getting my card. Too focused, as it turned out. I forgot to register for the event.

The tournament was at Sweetwater Country Club in Houston, where I had played many times in college. Because I knew my way around, I went in the pro shop entrance without checking in at the registration desk in the clubhouse. I was practicing on the range when fellow golfer, Michele Redman asked me if I had registered. "Please say yes, she said. I was scared to death so I ran to the tournament office and tried begging and pleading to no avail. I was disqualified from the event before play began and beat myself up about it for years.

I had to let go of my dream to finally break through. I took a job for a golf-luggage company last year, caddied for Rocky Thompson and Jim Feree on the Senior tour, and got in shape. With lower expectations, I got out of my own way long enough at Q school to earn my conditional card by four strokes.

As Blanche Dubois said in "A Street Car Named Desire", "I've always depended on the kindness of strangers. I'm indebted to many people for their support and sponsorship. Now it's time to pay them back."

Our first meeting came while walking across empty fairways of the Corning Country Club toward the parking lot. I had come straight from work to see what pros might be hanging around and also to socialize with members of the club.

"Hey mister! Do you belong to this club"? The salutation had shock value since there wasn't anyone I could see on the hole I was traversing. On the adjacent fairway was a short person carrying a bag and waving. She had the appearance of a caddy walking yardages but as I neared, I could recognize Lisa as a player.

"If you're a member, can you walk a couple of holes and give me some tips? Especially the greens, since these suckers have some tough reads. By the way, I'm Lisa Depaulo and I'm playing this tournament". We ran out of daylight, but not before I fell in love with her spirit. I even took vacation time the next day in order to be there for her opening round, playing under a Corning sponsor's exemption.

I rushed to see the first electronic scoring board only to be shocked when I saw her name listed in fourth place, under par early in the round. Her second round was a 78 and she missed the cut. I blame myself for not being there on Friday to offer support.

Lisa rededicated herself to achieving her goal and won exempt status at the 2003 Q school by finishing 12th at -5 and no round over par. She had partial sponsorship from her luggage company and free to let it fly. Weekly, I checked her scores only to see there were few cuts made. I know she gave her all and still has the feeling she can play with the best, just like I did.

BANQUETS AND STARS

Elmira's Sport Hall of Fame has been resurrected after years of mothballing. This event was similar to the mid winter Elmira Sports Banquet gathering but without the overhead. Because of inflated speaker fees and the lack of star quality available to generate ticket sales, the prime mid winter outing in Elmira has died. Salaries in all sports have eliminated the need for supportive income during the off season and no reason to battle snow storms to reach Elmira and their paycheck.

The major event was held for more than thirty years and the diverse roster of sports celebrities was impressive. Local athletes were included providing their fifteen minutes of fame, always boosting extra ticket sales needed to support the banquet. In the early days, there were a few mistakes made as to the master of ceremonies and I'll never forget the year Mel Allen was the MC.

The Mark Twain Hotel was a wonderful, historical place to house legendary people such as Mel. He was one of the most famous sports broadcasters of all time and had been the voice of the New York Yankees for many years. Even though I lived in Ohio, I was able to pick up his broadcasts occasionally and loved the differences between the Indian's long time announcer, Jimmy Dudley, and Allen. Mel would occasionally drop references to past heroes, mentioning Ruth and Gherig.

I knew the event was being held this particular night and couldn't resist stopping at the Twain bar to see who was hanging around. None of the featured guests were there except for Allen. He was surrounded by people and I didn't have a chance to make contact. The story in the paper the following day was amusing. Apparently, Mel had been over served and later provided a rambling, sometimes incoherent, performance to more than two hundred people. After attending many of the earlier banquets, I realized there was no reason to attend another unless there was one special guest and my family knew who this person was.

"Dad, guess who's going to be at the All Sports Banquet"? This was my daughter's greeting on our front porch before I could enter the house. It was mid January, the temperature ten below zero, and not hard to figure out who this mystery person would be. Once inside, Jeff offered the most unique challenge. "Dad, I'll believe all your bullshit as to whether you even played pro ball if Jim Palmer recognizes you."

I hid behind a large individual in the autograph line and when it was my turn, I threw down the 1969 Orioles radio and TV press guide which included both our profiles. "Sign this you old son of a bitch!" Jim's response was to jump up and give me a hug while a long line waited. We quickly shared information about what was going on in our lives and then it was time to part. Jeff just grinned from the hallway.

One of the banquets I did attend without my family was when Rocky Blier was a key note speaker. Our connection went back to the 1964 season in Appleton, Wisconsin and sticks in the memory.

Rocky was an all state star in three sports and Baltimore wanted to sign him desperately before any college could lock him up via scholarship. This was professional baseball and they were going to dangle money unavailable from NCAA regulated programs.

I was Rocky's personal tutor for practices because I was a starter only working every fifth day. My control was perfect and, more importantly, delivered batting practice pitches at the required speed and location for showcasing his talent in a positive way. Baltimore had put me in a difficult position since I was being told to do something that potentially could be harmful to my arm and career by throwing multiple days between starts.

Rocky powered everything I fed him in all directions and out of the park often. One of the toughest things to do as a professional pitcher is to throttle back from what is capable. Adjusting the velocity upward to real game conditions would have shown him lacking and in locker room conversations, I could sense baseball was not his game. Still, it was exciting to be this close to the person since he was a local athlete who had potential, even if it wasn't in my sport.

Blier's Tavern was a great combination of food, drink, atmosphere, and Rocky's dad behind the bar playing host most of the time. One exceptionally cold Saturday afternoon I decided to stop and be warmed by the usual weekend sports crowd. I was overshadowed only by Rocky in this establishment. Blier's tavern could have been "Cheers" due to the diversity of the patrons.

Rocky's dad was called away to the phone, coming back visibly agitated about something. Someone asked, "Anything wrong?" His response was, "It's that god damned kid of mine. He said some alum called and told him, "Look out the window". The bastard bought him a Mustang convertible and parked it out front of the frat house with the keys in the glove compartment." Most were impressed with this generous gift, but I knew what was coming.

"I told him he couldn't keep it and he got pissed at me. I reminded him of the NCAA's strict rules and if he got caught, it would be the end of his scholarship and his football career." Rocky never drove the car, pop knew better. Rocky went on to a NFL career after being the 18th pick of the Pittsburgh Steelers in the football draft and was the only one to survive from that level or below.

Blier was drafted into the army and served in Viet Nam. During combat he was shot in the left leg and had a grenade explode under his right foot, blowing a portion away. Upon release from duty he was awarded a forty per cent disability because of these injuries. The drive to succeed was immeasurable when he reported to football summer camp.

Rocky became the starting fullback for the Steelers in 1974 and played during the period where the team won four Super Bowl titles in six years. Even though he was primarily a blocking back, he gained a thousand yards one season along with Franco Harris. After retiring, Blier developed into one of the countries best motivational speakers and now commands large appearance fees.

HOW TO NEGOTIATE A CONTRACT

My contract, for draft purposes, had been assigned to the Elmira club for the 1967 season. This did not mean you were going to play at this level, it only established the pecking order in the organization. The major league gamble was no one else would risk a draft choice to pick up your contract at a higher level. The minor league general manager was assigned to initiate the process and my letter came from Gary Girmindl. Here is my second response after the refusal of a counter offer on my part.

Dear Gary,

Enclosed, please find my contract with the Elmira Club for $850 per month. The contract is unsigned as I don't believe this to be satisfactory. Someone seems to have missed the point I was trying to make concerning last years record as far as salary negotiations are concerned. I am enclosing several articles from papers in both Kennewick, Washington and Lewiston, Idaho.

The first is an article by Cal Ripken giving an evaluation of our club in Appleton for the 1964 season and just why we won the second half championship and then the playoffs. According to Cal, the organization knew I could potentially have a slow start because of the short time spent in spring training. Since I ended up leading all the pitchers and won the MVP, this must account for something.

The second clipping is the complete second half averages of both the Lewiston club and the Atoms. As you can see, my record and earned run average are both quite good. My ERA is .01 higher than the leading starting pitcher, Bill McMahon. I also pitched the second most amount of innings that half. This is what I am basing my demands upon for I feel these records reflect my performance this year.

As far as my not having played at Elmira, I do not believe this is my fault at all. I just play the game and leave the player movement up to Baltimore. In 1964, at one point my record was 8-0, leading the league in almost everything and yet I wasn't moved one notch upward. You are quite a ways off base when you state a player's placement depends greatly on your spring training showing. In the three years I have gone to spring training with AA and down, I have never seen a ballplayer advanced from Thomasville to Daytona Beach to train with the Rochester club. The only direction is always down or out, never up. A good friend of mine once had a string of 33 scoreless innings at Thomasville and ended up going to Stockton to play.

I don't see how you can quote a good AA salary as every organization pays differently. One organization I have in mind had several players on its team who were making almost twice as much as the highest paid member of our team.

You need not bother to tell me to, "analyze my situation" for with my past record in professional baseball, I would have no difficulty negotiating with any of the other 19 major league organizations and if Baltimore does not feel I am worth this much, then they surely must not hold any future plans for me and my release would be very greatly appreciated.

Yours sincerely,

Tim Sommer

This is a document unseen for almost forty years until finding it buried in a box in our basement. I know this was the foundation for Lou Gorman offering both a minor league pitching coaching job and the general manager's position for one of their lower classifications after I retired.

Since I never joined Elmira in 1966 due to Darrell Johnson, I negotiated once again with Gary the following year. My gain from previous negotiations was a contract

114

making $1100 per month. This time, since I had a record of 11-17, Gary's initial letter sounded as if I had leprosy and shouldn't have anything to do with the Orioles organization. But they were willing to take a chance if I accepted the same salary as last year.

My patience was exhausted with this process. After losing thirteen games by one run, an ERA in the top ten and leading all lower minor leagues in innings pitched, I failed to come up with adequate words. Instead, I returned my contract with the dollar amount crossed off and a large "NO".

In addition to this rejection was something extra. On heavy construction paper I drew several primitive objects. One was six stick figures shown in diminishing heights and below these, "FAMILY". Next I drew a dollar bill with wings and put "INFLATION" below this. Everything I drew thereafter was pictorially related to my demands. There was no response for weeks meaning my career might be over.

One day an official letter from the Orioles arrived. If I were gone it wouldn't be so bad because I was living in California and life would be good there. When I dared to look at the small block where salary was noted, there was a shock. It was the $1500 I had asked for. I signed and returned the contract immediately with a return signature request. Only after settling into the season and getting to know Gary better did I learn the amusing story as to the ease of this contract acceptance.

Gary opened my envelope and pulled the contract out along with the construction paper insert. I had carefully folded this heavy paper into an elaborate paper air plane that was designed to fly in long, looping circles rather than the straight ahead kind. He shook the envelope looking for a letter, but there was none.

As Gary tells it, he was so angry at my response the paper was crumpled and thrown into his waste basket. But as he thought about a report to Baltimore on our impasse he began to understand my humor and gave a recommendation, 'give this kid the money." He couldn't wait to meet up with me.

There is more to having a great season than the won loss side. It is how you react to demands for personal services with little definition under the simple language of our minor league contracts. In Elmira, this meant we could be ordered to appear at a clothing store with only one day's notice. There was no consideration this might be a scheduled day off and plans had been made by families to relax and enjoy a rare moment together.

Girmindl was lacking in understanding many details about his job and one Sunday afternoon turned out to be classic. If I hadn't bailed him out there could have been a riot. I'm sure this is why he stuffed the ballot box in my favor for the most popular player voting the following year. My prize was a GE electric carving knife presented before a home crowd of 1000 people.

Communications broke down between Gary and the general manager of the Yankee's club in Binghamton. Our published schedule said we had a home game this Sunday afternoon starting at 2 pm. It was Bat Day and two thousand youngsters were in the stands armed with eighteen inch replicas of Louisville Sluggers. It was unusually hot and muggy and most parents would rather have been somewhere else. We were gathered together on this Sunday, all except for the opposing team.

Apparently, the Binghamton GM had requested a time change to a night game the month before because of a conflict and Gary agreed. "No problem, I'll take care of it." This meant coordinating with everyone. New tickets to print, vendors supplying food, time to turn on the lights and most importantly, telling his team when to arrive. Nothing had taken place and Gary was in the worst position of his career when he entered our clubhouse looking for help. The game was an hour late and bats were being pounded on every available seat.

"Will someone come out and sign bats until we can put a game together?" This request had been made to a veteran team only two steps from the major leagues. I volunteered with no hesitation. "Gary, where do you want me"? He handed me three magic markers and we went to the rear of the home club dugout roof where fans could be funneled for an orderly signing.

I signed bats for more than two hours and only quit when the Binghamton team arrived for the game. They had a collection of players rounded up from apartments, picnics and swimming pools and five pitchers were in the starting lineup. There is no memory as to the outcome. I was worn out and extremely happy to be a right handed pitcher and a left handed signer.

LOCAL FLAVOR

When salaries for major league players started their exponential climb there was a corresponding popularity shift toward the minor leagues. Increasing ticket prices put pressure on the average family wanting to see a major league game on a regular basis. I remember a story in Sporting News and the hypocrisy within a press release issued by the Pittsburgh Pirates describing ticket prices for the upcoming season. The spin was, free agency would have little impact and they were holding the line. What they didn't include in this statement was popcorn would be twice as expensive.

Currently, the best entertainment value for a sporting event is found in minor league baseball. New parks have been built and a family can still afford the cost. You really can get an autograph and smile from a young player who doesn't know if he will survive. But gone forever are the old parks since most were built more than fifty years ago. Almost all had their own very distinct personalities.

The park in Pittsfield was angled to follow a river bank, making for irregular out field distances. The one in Bakersfield was built backwards because of a land dispute, so the setting sun during a night game was directly in the eyes of the batter. Along with unique parks came characters unusual in their own right.

Lewiston, Idaho in the sixties was still a frontier town. While browsing Woolworth's one afternoon I saw a full headdress above the racks moving around. There was a reservation near the city and a chieftain was shopping alone. Every night another member of his tribe took up residence in the front row wrapped in a beautiful blanket. The disconcerting element was he never moved a muscle for the entire game and you couldn't help but focus on this person.

Though I could usually block out distractions, he became difficult to ignore while looking for my catcher's signals. His stoic nature continued until the stands were almost empty and time to carefully fold his blanket before returning to the reservation.

The most unusual character was Abe Lincoln in Decatur, Illinois. He was a brilliant electronic engineer whose mind had snapped, locking him into the past as Lincoln. Every night he arrived in costume looking better than the portrait on a five dollar bill. He was positioned directly behind home plate so there was no avoiding his movements. As you started the windup, Abe would wave his arms in a random manner and the combination of these movements and his costume did affect some during the course of a game.

The beautiful part came after the final game of each three game set. We were aboard our bus when Abe would enter to say his goodbyes. It was always the same and to show our level of respect for the person, nobody ever said anything demeaning. We waited for the speech and it was always the same.

After removing his stove pipe hat Abe offered, "Gentlemen, I want to thank everyone for a wonderful game and more importantly, your professionalism. You all are a credit to baseball". Our response was always, "Thanks Abe, see you next time in town". Lincoln then left the bus walking alone into the darkness.

Elmira had a colorful character roaming the stands during the game from center section to the bleachers lining the foul lines. What made him distinctive was the voice. Even with several thousand people in the stands his whereabouts were known as he moved about the park, never sitting.

Whenever one of our pitchers needed a little extra help he would yell out, "Put some zookum on the ball!" If more magic were required, he would somehow work his way into the opposing team's bullpen and deliver his voodoo behind their bench. Most times he was chased away immediately, but the message had been delivered. Our crowd would be infected by his enthusiasm and by the end of the game there was a chant to put some "zookum" on whatever you were going to throw.

Another person few knew anything about was Bob Bolger. He was our public address announcer, blessed with a voice both commanding and rich. Unfortunately Bob had a bit of a problem with alcohol, producing some memorable moments at Dunn Field. During one night game the crowd heard this report from a major league game. "The score between the Yankees and Phillies in the seventh is, 3-2. This was decades before inter league play and Bob had put together two pieces of Western Union tape without realizing his error. Those of us in the bullpen could laugh out loud without being heard.

Bolger's most famous gaffe came after leaving the mike open one night. For several minutes, two thousand people heard him rambling on, belching and delivering a classic. One of our players hit a shot down the left field line producing a tough call for the umpire as he moved into position. His decision was foul ball, sending Bob into motion high above the stands. "That son of a bitch is blind. I'm three hundred feet away and could see it was fair. Where the hell do they get these guys? My eighty year old mother has better eyesight than that bastard!" Bob was immediately silenced, never returning to his duties that night.

Several years later I heard and observed his same type of mistake at the national level when Dizzy Dean and Pee Wee Reese were teaming together for the NBC Game of the Week on a Saturday afternoon. Dean offered, "Pardner there the two lovebirds are, he's kissing her on the strikes and she's kissing him on the balls". The camera had focused on two young people who hadn't sought refuge during a rain delay of a Yankee's game and were involved in romantic foreplay oblivious to everyone. Another Dean memory is when Dizzy slid into second and was carried off to a local hospital after being knocked out. "X-Rays of Dean's Head Shows Nothing" was the headline the next day.

Over the years I learned how varied Bob's career had been prior to arriving in Elmira. Looking at the person, it seemed unlikely he could have been an associate producer for the original Today Show on NBC or in a major movie.

One of the most memorable movies I ever saw at the age of nine was, "Johnny One Eye" with Pat O'Brien as the star. Written by legendary newspaper reporter and writer Damon Runyon, this was a low budget film that moved on to be a classic.

One afternoon I mentioned this movie and Bob described O'Brien's death scene perfectly. After O'Brien shot the real bad guy and was dying from his own wounds, there was a squad of cops who entered the room. He was one of the policemen surrounding the body but had no dialogue as the movie ended with a fadeout. Bolger was the real deal, his bloopers were classics and I was privileged to know this person.

I broke camp to play for the Tri City Atoms in 1965 traveling alone in my 1960 Corvair. This car may have been labeled a death trap by Ralph Nader, but it was my only transportation for the next two seasons. When the movie "Christine' came out in 1983 about a crazed car acting on it's own, I realized there were personalities involved in car ownership.

Driving well into the night my first day on the road placed me in Selma, Alabama. I awoke the next morning thinking only about the upcoming season in Kennewick, Washington. Near the motel was a diner surrounded by cars, indicating an excellent breakfast must be inside. Just before entering the diner I bought a newspaper and noticed something strange. All the people seated in the front booths were looking at me through the windows as I approached and everyone had stopped eating.

It was early morning and I wanted to head west as soon as possible so my order was scrambled eggs and coffee. The waitress came with the coffee, sliding it down the counter with liquid landing in my lap. Only when I opened the paper did I know what was happening and why every person had stopped eating or talking.

"FREEDOM RIDER KILLED BY KKK". This was a headline across the entire front page. My Corvair had Ohio plates and everything I owned was crammed into the interior. This included an ironing board cut down to fit between the front windshield and rear window. Shifting was easy underneath this appliance.

A group of Michigan people, mostly from Detroit, had arrived in Selma to participate in what was intended to be one of the first peaceful marches in America supporting black equality. This was a decade after Rosa Parks created history by refusing to give up her seat one evening on a bus in Montgomery, Alabama. She was coming home from work and her feet were aching from standing all day. Rosa was ordered to give up her seat to a white passenger and she refused, resulting in her arrest. The Supreme Court settled this issue and the change in America was coming.

The Klan had killed a woman the night before and the occupants of the diner just knew I had to be part of her group. Trying not to show fear, I drank what was left of my coffee waiting for conversation to resume. The exit was ten feet to the left and when my presence was less notable I prepared to leave. Coffee was twenty cents and I threw a dollar bill on the counter in front of my waitress. We had a stare down for a few seconds but she had the momentum and it was time to move on.

Selma, Alabama was a small town of 30,000 located in Dallas County, where only 1% of eligible blacks were registered to vote. The registrar's office was open twice a month and often workers came in late, took long lunch breaks and went home early. Few blacks passed the required test for registration, stumbling over some words such as "constitutionality". Whites met attempts by blacks to register with strong resistance. Under orders from Sheriff Jim Clark, pictures of blacks lining up to register were taken and these people were asked what their employers would think of the pictures. Police beat people who tried to bring food and water to those in line for registration.

In early 1965, civil rights activists began to protest in Selma in order to bring attention to racial injustice. These protests were often met by violence from the local sheriff's department and one march on February 17 ended with the shooting of one of the protesters, Jimmy Lee Jackson, who died several days later from his wounds.

Those demonstrating felt there couldn't be support in a town as small as Selma for too long, so it turned its attention to other areas. On February 17, a night march was planned from a church to the jail in nearby Marion. Police spread rumors that participants would break someone out of jail. At the conclusion of the march, police attacked the marchers and Jimmie Lee Jackson, a black Vietnam veteran, was shot as he tried to protect his mother. He died seven days later.

Martin Luther King, who had been preaching in Atlanta on "Bloody Sunday," immediately started making plans for a new march. He called on people from all over the country to join him in Selma. To prevent any further violence, the marchers wanted to get a court order prohibiting the police from stopping the march. The federal judge who heard the case often sided with civil rights workers, but he issued a restraining order, saying the march could not take place.

On March 7, 600 peaceful protesters left Browns Chapel Methodist Church in Selma intent on marching the 50 miles to Montgomery as a memorial to Jackson and to protest for voter's rights. As they crossed the Pettus bridge, they were met by a column of State troopers and local volunteer officers of the sheriff's office who blocked their path. When told to reverse their direction and refused, they were attacked with nightsticks and tear gas driving the marchers back over the bridge and to the church. The initial violent incident happened in full view of the nation's press but they had been held back as the marchers retreated into the black community, where the violence continued for some time.

March 21, fourteen days after Bloody Sunday, the marchers crossed over the Edmund Pettus Bridge and kept going. President Johnson had federalized the Alabama National Guard to give the marchers protection. The march took five days and there was no violence until the night of my arrival in Selma.

When the march entered Montgomery, it was 25,000 people strong and included many heroes of the civil rights movement, such as Martin Luther King, Rosa Parks and John

Lewis. It was a triumphant moment, a return to where the movement had started ten years earlier.

King told his audience, "However difficult the moment, however frustrating the hour, it will not be long, because truth crushed to the earth will rise again....How long? Not long. Because mine eyes have seen the glory of the coming of the Lord." One of the greatest statements in history and truly a day for celebration.

That night, Viola Liuzzo, a white 39 year old mother of five, wife of a Detroit Teamster and the only white woman murdered during the civil rights movement, was shot in the head and killed by a car full of Klansmen while returning from Montgomery. Liuzzo's death came at a pivotal moment in the movement because President Johnson had been fighting an uphill battle to push the Voter's Rights Act through Congress. Historians of the era say her murder provided the final piece of leverage that won Johnson approval of the Act, which forever changed the U.S. political landscape.

After leaving the diner I was cruising and all thoughts were focused on how great my season was going to be. The Interstate Highway system was less than one third built and most of the projects in the South always seemed to be behind the rest of the country. There were no additional problems until I hit Mississippi.

I had to make a quick move to avoid the carcass of a dead mule with its legs protruding onto the highway slightly. Rigor mortis had set in so the legs were perfectly stiff. Fortunately there was no oncoming traffic and, blessed with youthful reflexes, I swerved in time avoiding an accident.

Two miles ahead was a Highway Patrol outpost. Everywhere else in the country these were impressive structures showing authority. This a cement block building housing a front desk area and one room off the side. Since I had parked in front of the entrance, my Ohio plate was visible to the person behind the desk. It was my civic duty to report the potential road hazard.

"I want to report a dead mule back up the road that could cause an accident." The sergeant took awhile to respond. "Son, I suggest you get your Yankee ass back in your Yankee car and keep heading west. We take care of everything ourselves and don't need your help. Do you understand?" I couldn't wait to get to Washington. Surely the rest of the country couldn't be like this.

The trip west was an incredible learning experience providing first hand knowledge as to America's size. Driving across Texas became lonely and I began offering poor imitations of what I thought a bull might sound like to see if one cow's head would turn. To me, this was ultimate boredom because not one animal gave me a glance.

THE TRAP WAS SET

Despite a career best season the year before, I returned to Elmira in 1968 because of pitching talent ahead. Although this bothered me, I was able to accept my placement. Five years experience and an honest assessment of competition convinced me the goal was achievable and only a matter of time.

Because of professional baseball's popularity in Elmira, plus the Oriole affiliation, there was a strong relationship between players and fans. They were watching those next in line who might possibly move on to the parent club. This is the fun part of minor league baseball and continues today. Fans were afforded close contact with players throughout the community.

I was now the team closer and every game was a possible save for me. Our starting pitcher ran into trouble during the eighth and my adrenalin started to flow.

A single voice started yelling at the top of his lungs. "Bring in Sommer!" It was so timely and comical, my mates in the bullpen started to razz me. "Is that guy on your pass list and how much did you pay him for the cheer leading?"

My newest and most vocal fan was Jim Cassidy. We had met the previous evening at a tiny tavern several blocks from the park. This watering hole couldn't hold more than thirty people and it's only attraction during summer evenings was being close to the park. It was also within three hundred feet of my rented room.

It was difficult to be inconspicuous because of the informal dress code for professional baseball players of this era. Alpaca sweaters and Sansabelt tailored slacks didn't fit in with locals, but Jim didn't hesitate approaching me. "What the hell are you doing in here?" His question was delivered with a smile and an outstretched hand. Forty years later we remain the best of friends and our families have grown up together in a way that few have the opportunity to achieve.

The premier bar in Elmira for those in their early twenties was "Bill's". This tavern was adjacent to Elmira College and on most nights difficult to walk through due to crowds. My ego was stroked every time because of our celebrity status and it was the best possible chance to meet a local girl hoping to get next to a player. The crowd this night was greater than normal, requiring an effort to reach the bar. I found a small area where the view was unobstructed and spotted a friendly face.

Chris Douer was a telephone operator I met the previous season in Elmira with an immediate attraction because of her height. Chris reminded me of the first person I dated at Ohio University, "Dolly" Swope. The connection was both were taller than me. Dolly was the center for the OU women's basketball team but slightly uncoordinated. Part of our dating pattern was to shoot hoops in the women's gym and when I would dunk she stopped talking to me. Chris was taller than Dolly but shared the same lament about tall men dating short women.

"Hi Tim, I want you to meet a good friend of mine, Mary Slavin. We both work at the phone company." After our introduction, Mary said little and I wondered what brought her out this night. Suddenly, Chris got up from the booth declaring, "There's someone over there I want to talk to." And then we were alone.

I remember the slow buildup in our conversation. It was like the startup of a gyroscope on board a cruise ship and until it reaches maximum rotation the ship can tilt a little. Despite the collateral noise, I heard nothing other than what Mary said for the rest of the night.

We stayed until closing and since I had no car Mary offered a ride to my apartment. This was awkward because she was aware of a past relationship with the daughter of my landlords. We were leaving on a nine day road trip the following morning and I had volunteered to help paint her parent's bathroom upon returning. This offer was sincere and should have indicated how much I wanted to be with her again.

Panic set in after returning from the road trip since I couldn't remember her last name of Slavin. I found a phone book and spent two hours looking at all the names, hoping a trigger would be pulled. Our game was over and I returned to Bill's with the hope Mary might be there. She had never been there before our first meeting and I doubted I would find her again. It was curious why I worried. This was my sixth year of professional baseball and there had only been one relationship prior equaling these feelings.

As I was about to leave I saw Mary heading for the bar. She returned to her table and I picked a spot where my presence couldn't be seen. It took more nerve to approach than standing on the mound. She was too polite to question what happened to my broken bathroom painting promise. I measured every past relationship while we were talking and came to the conclusion it was time to stop searching.

WINTER BALL WAS A VACATION

As a reward for my 1968 season, I was selected to play winter ball in the Florida Instructional League. This was a platform for up and coming prospects, plus those whose major league credentials had slipped due to injury or poor performance. Since I hadn't played in the bigs, I put myself in the first category. Our manager was Cal Ripken, Sr and the roster had Don Baylor, Curt Blefary, Rich Coggins, Terry Crowley, Ron Dunn, Roger Freed, Bobby Grich, John Montague, Jim Palmer and Al Severinson, all of whom made major league clubs at various times in their career.

Winter league baseball was the ultimate luxury for a player no matter whether it was the Florida Instructional League, Puerto Rico or any Latin American country. You had been identified as someone the organization had tapped for a reason. It was an invisible chevron to be displayed on your uniform the following spring training providing a major psychological edge over both those remaining and those to come. My 1.16 ERA was the reason for the invitation to the major league camp in the next few months, coupled with the possibility of the first ever player's strike in the history of the game.

Marvin Miller, head of the Major League Player's Association, and the owners were $800,000 apart on the annual pension contributions and a world apart on other issues. The owners wanted to keep the number of years to vest at five and rejected Miller's contention money had to keep pace with TV revenue. Miller did some math and shared the analysis with the players,

The current pension deal required each of the twenty clubs to contribute $205,000 per year. The new offer only increased the per club contribution to $212,500. That was just $125 more per player. Running in place was really sliding backward. Miller put it to a vote. The result was 491-7, against. They were ready to hold out and I could have a shot at the bigs.

Baltimore had contracted with a motel featuring efficiency apartments so we could survive without having to eat every meal in a restaurant. Plus, there was daily maid service to clean up any mess in the kitchen I might make. Word had spread about my culinary skills and often there were visitors around dinner time enjoying whatever I had put together.

The most interesting character on our team had to be Curt Blefary. Curt was born in Brooklyn and originally signed with the Yankees, but sold to Baltimore while still in the minors. He was named American League Rookie of the Year as an outfielder for the Orioles in 1965 when he hit .260 with 22 home runs and 70 RBI's. His nickname, "Clank", was given by Frank Robinson, in part for his below average fielding abilities. In an effort to keep his bat in the lineup, Baltimore shifted him from outfield to catcher and on April 27, 1968 he caught Tom Phoebus' no hitter against the Red Sox.

Curt and I developed a friendship upon meeting for no reason other than we enjoyed each other's company. It didn't matter he was Baltimore's second AL Rookie of the year in franchise history having hit 82 home runs for the Orioles over the past four seasons. I was someone he never heard of but we both looked at life in a humorous way, the only way to survive the pressures of professional baseball.

During the second week of camp, I noticed Curt slipping away into our clubhouse at precisely the same time each day, returning five minutes later. After the third day I confronted him. "What the heck are you doing when you go back into the clubhouse? You can't be that regular so you have to take a crap precisely at eleven."

"I've got a big check coming from the Orioles and I don't want my wife to get her hands on it. I got my land lady watching the mail and she's going to send it to me." How he convinced this person to commit mail fraud was understandable, because Curt was absolutely charming.

The next day he repeated the routine but there was a grin on his face when we made eye contact, and he gave me a discreet thumb up signal. Nothing was mentioned until the mail arrived a few days later and Blefary offered an invitation to a select few for a night of partying on him.

We went to the best night club Clearwater had to offer and the drinks were on Curt for the evening. The night was electric because of the quality of the band and a large number of single women. A buzz started when people learned there were seven professional baseball players in attendance. Only Blefary had the big league credentials, but we all were able to walk the walk and talk the talk.

Last call for drinks arrived and our group had swelled to more than twenty. The most beautiful were sitting on each side of Curt, a blond and a red head. They matched his good looks and it made sense when the threesome stood up and prepared to leave. "Boys, I'll see you later but I don't know when that will be. Tell Rip not to get nervous." This was the last we saw of Blefary for two days.

When Curt did show up, there were no questions asked, at least not in front of the club. I'm sure Rip had to report to the front office in the same manner as to Dalkowski's actions three years previous. The big difference between the two was, Baltimore was able to trade Blefary to Houston after winter ball for Mike Cuellar in what is recognized as one of the best trades made in the history of the Orioles. Cuellar led the club in victories with a 23-11 record and went on to have four twenty game seasons.

I was bothered by Curt's cavalier attitude about his career, but because he was so likable, you just believed he was able to accept his fate head on. The best quote came when he described his batting average of .200 the past season with the Orioles.

"If you hit .199 everyone will say he just had a bad year, he's much better than that. If you hit .200 you've crossed the line and aren't a prospect and then you're gone." Years later this same philosophy became known as the "Mendoza Line", for a similar statistical position and a debate as to the origin. It has now become part of America's lexicon used for describing someone on the bubble of survival in professional baseball.

After a full season with the Astros, Blefary was used as a part time player by the Yankees, Athletics and Padres. Upon retiring in 1972, he tried unsuccessfully to continue his career in baseball as a coach. He worked as a sheriff, bartender, truck driver, and later owned a night club. In 1995 he acknowledged his long time drinking problem and asked for help from B.A.T (Baseball Assistance Team), an organization formed to help down and out baseball people.

Curt died in Pompano Beach, Florida at age 57 in 2001. His last wish was to be buried in Baltimore's Memorial Stadium. Although the park was nearly demolished when he passed away, his wife Lana was able to honor his request to scatter his ashes in Memorial Stadium. The Babe Ruth Museum supplied the home plate used in the final game at the stadium and located it in the precise spot where it had been used. The ceremony was held on May 24, 2001. "He loved Baltimore, and he loved his fans, said his wife. "He was a lifelong student of the game." In telling this story over the last decade, not a person has been able to give me the name of the 1965 AL Rookie of the Year.

RACIAL PROBLEMS IN AMERICA

I was called up to Rochester toward the end of the 1968 season, joining the club in Louisville, Kentucky. Since the ball park was within the State fair grounds, well out of town, the cab ride sent me there instead of the hotel. There was a feeling, on my part, if I were able to impress this night there could be a return to the airport and a flight to Baltimore.

Reality set in after the game when our bus was stopped five blocks from the center of the city and our destination, the Brown Hotel. This area was cordoned off due to rioting and we had to sprint the rest of the way. I was the only one burdened with two suitcases and sporadic gunfire could be heard in the direction we were headed.

Jerry Herron turned and saw me struggling to keep up. We knew each other from the previous season and because he was the largest player on our club, this combination might have saved my life. Herron left the main body coming back to grab my suitcases along with the encouragement, "Come on, we've got to keep up or they'll pick us off!"

It was a strange sensation checking into such a storied hotel as the Brown with the front desk staff acting as if nothing were going on. They were true professionals, but didn't have to run a quarter mile dodging potential snipers.

The Brown was elegant and made one feel he really was close to the major leagues. It opened in 1923, registering David Lloyd George, former Prime Minister of England, as its first guest. Three years later, the head chef invented the famed sandwich, "Hot Brown". Lily Pons let her pet lion club roam free in her suite and Al Jolson got into a fight in the hotel's English Grill, declaring later that makeup would cover his shiner before he went on for a performance in the

Brown Theater. Due to the age of the hotel, rooms were small by 1960's standards, but classy.

It took an hour before I was able to calm down and call Mary in Elmira to tell about this day's events. My window was open and sounds of the night were coming in, along with cool breezes, when she answered. Within seconds, a series of shots occurred near the hotel and she innocently asked, "What's that, firecrackers?" The tensions within me caused the response, "Don't you have a clue as to what's going on around the country? Those are gunshots!" I moved the phone to a position in the room where a ricochet wouldn't hit me and only then could we talk calmly.

The following year a three game series with Norfolk was canceled because of rioting. The city was shutdown with no movement after dark allowed. We were told not to step foot on the sidewalk in front of the hotel since this would constitute a violation of orders and the inference one could be shot by any enforcing agency. For three days, we only moved between rooms, the restaurant and the bar. For the blacks on the club, it was only between rooms and the restaurant.

Since we were young and mostly ignorant as to what was occurring nationally we saw this as the perfect opportunity for an extended party. We had to decide on what time to wake up, what time to eat and what time to head for the bar. To the hotel's credit, they never ran out of beer and we were able to enjoy the company of Dorrel Norman Elvert Herzog, aka, Whitey Herzog, one of baseball's greatest characters who was trapped along with our team.

Herzog had spent fifteen years as an active player bouncing around the major leagues with no real success, his last year being 1963 with the Tigers. On this trip he was functioning as a scout for the New York Mets assigned to evaluate talent at the AAA level. Four years from this point he began a long, successful, colorful, managing career starting with Texas, concluding in 1990 with St. Louis. His overall winning percentage was .532 and was named NL Manager of the Year in 1985.

Never again would I have a chance to hear baseball stories like this man offered. He held court in the bar from about ten each evening until they kicked us out. Since there were no enforced legal hours, often we would leave at three am. Never was there a problem as to time since our tip monies were substantial and we repeated the process three straight days.

Whitey is legendary not only as to his record as a manager, but also for media quotes. Here are my favorites.

"Baseball has been good to me since I quit trying to play it."

"I'm not buddy-buddy with the players. If they need a buddy, let them buy a dog."

"The only thing bad about winning the pennant is that you have to manage the All-Star game the next year. I'd rather go fishing for three days".

"The only way to make money as a manager is to win in one place, get fired and hired somewhere else."

"We need just two players to be a contender. Just Babe Ruth and Sandy Koufax."

"You sweat out the free agent thing in November, then you make the trades in December. Then you struggle to sign the guys left in January and in February I get down to sewing all the new names on the uniforms."

Even though six black players were on the roster, there was no racial tension in the clubhouse despite what has happening nationally. This represents the quality of professional baseball as a team sport at this time. We were playing the game as if we were still kids and our fields could have been in a ghetto, cane field, or cow pasture.

Earlier in the season, prior to the call up to Rochester, my National Guard unit came within hours of being activated to protect Buffalo. The call to duty came through the Pioneer's front office during a game and my orders to report were delivered by our bat boy.

What a transition from sitting in the bullpen to an instructional drill on how to provide crowd control by pointing a bayonet at the throat of the person you were trying to move. If you had to stab this person and the bayonet became lodged between bones, the proper procedure was to fire a round into the body. The recoil would assist in the knife's removal and you could move forward. We received a stand down minutes before departure and I couldn't wait to turn in the ammunition. My job was to throw bullets, not fire them.

YOU CAN'T PREDICT FAME

Thurman Munson was a star football, basketball and baseball player while playing for Lehman High School in Canton, Ohio. He attended Kent State University earning All America honors and in June of 1968, Munson was the New York Yankee's top pick in the amateur Free Agent Draft, receiving a $75,000 signing bonus.

Thurman's starting salary was the minimum $500 per month, only for the playing season. He began his career against us on a Sunday afternoon in Elmira and this was my first chance to promote Mid American Conference quality of players. For the Yankees to start him at this classification was validation for my bragging about our conference.

I sought Munson out during batting practice hoping to establish a bond. We both had been born in Canton, attended a MAC school and I was a veteran welcoming him to professional baseball. Our introduction was short, but comfortable, and neither of us knew the eventual outcome of our careers.

Bobby Darwin was handling first base coaching duties and couldn't wait to return to the dugout after the first inning. "This guy doesn't have a clue as to what he's doing. He's catching so wide open I can call every pitch without getting out of the coaching box. Let's set up some signals." This declaration was devastating to me from an ego standpoint, as this All American was being accused of baseball fraud.

Bobby set up voice signals for each pitch thrown since it was easy to intercept, translate, and pass on to the batter. Darwin transferred information by using the hitter's first name for a fastball and last name for something slower. Our three game series was so lopsided, there had to be a residual effect on every Binghamton pitcher's salary negotiations during the winter just because of Thurman's ignorance.

One month later, we played against Munson in his home park for a three game series. Thurman had corrected his problem and exhibited a leadership quality that wasn't there in Elmira. He was in control of calling the game but also player positioning in the field. There was no looking into the dugout to see what his manager wanted, he was in charge and both teams knew this.

After the game, I asked Thurman about the correction in his catching technique since we could now talk at length, both personally and professionally.

"Did you know what you were doing your first game?" This question was too vague and I went on to explain. "We were calling pitches because you were catching wide open and Darwin could see every signal." Munson took awhile to analyze what he heard and then a smile formed.

"I knew something was wrong because pro ball couldn't be that far off from college. There were some of our pitchers really pissed at me for the reputation, bonus money, and starting at this level. There wasn't a single coach along the way who saw this until an old Yankee scout saw me for the first home series. This is the way I grew up catching." We shook hands and, after leaving the field, I didn't feel there were any professional ethics violated.

CAUGHT IN A WEB

Every player has an escape clause for summer relationships. The transient nature of the job is the most convenient excuse but sometimes other factors can cause plans to change. This happened to me while playing winter ball in 1968 after dating Mary this summer in Elmira. The Vietnam conflict caused hardships and decisions about one's career.

It would have been easy to flee to Canada but not one player did. Professional athletes had to scramble for a position with the services to minimize time away from their sport and often politics were involved. The greater your value to the organization, the easier it was for a player to find himself entered into a Reserve program. This meant only six months of active duty and then back to the brass ring chase. I had no political stance whether the war was right or wrong, I just wanted to play baseball and succeed.

It was humorous when the battalion commander called me into his office prior to mustering out after six months of training. His pitch was to sign me up for a career in the Army because of my "unlimited leadership skills". This is the same person who, upon learning of my photography background, commissioned me to develop pornographic pictures he had taken with a self timer camera of him and his Viet Nam mistress. Somehow, I couldn't tie logic into our differing viewpoints about my future.

We were staying in a small two floor efficiency motel when a minimal hurricane came through Clearwater during winter ball. Our team combined single with married, including Cal Ripken and his family. The evacuation notice was not mandatory so only married players and their families left the beach to be relocated at the Clearwater high school gymnasium. Wisely, the rest of us prepared for the approaching storm with assurances we had enough beer to survive.

All night we watched radar on television and only left our safe haven to stand in the middle of the hurricane eye as it passed over. Direct sunlight was above and objects were swirling in a half mile circle. It was surreal to see an aluminum rowboat, uprooted trees and dislodged fish moving horizontally. We only retreated when the back side made it dangerous to stay. For twenty four hours we had a full blast party surrounded with a "Superman" cloak of invincibility. No matter what came down, we were going to survive and be stronger for this experience.

The hurricane produced an odd series of events. Those who went inland to the gym, including the Ripken family, were rained upon after a major portion of the roof was blown away. The rest of us had a good time and far better stories to tell. We were truly concerned for the well being of our Oriole family as they fled, but we knew it was going to be a great party opportunity.

As winter ball came closer to conclusion, I realized there might be no chance for finding employment before spring training. Most players found themselves in the same position each year and decisions about whether to continue were constantly on their minds.

I felt somewhat secure in the belief my position with Shell Chemical in California was available. My coworkers were excited about having rubbed elbows with a professional athlete and were looking forward to hear my stories. I had the support of everyone despite almost causing the facility to be destroyed because of one little oversight on my part. I didn't know the skull and crossbones on a fifty five gallon drum of some chemical really meant anything.

One week before departing Clearwater, I made a confirming call to my supervisor at Shell to align the small details. His voice on the phone was strained and I thought there was some personal crisis in his life. What came next was shocking.

"Tim, I don't know how to tell you this, but your job isn't available". Even though we had a strong relationship, these were tense moments. I asked, "What happened"? His answer shocked my white, 60's, Midwestern, conservative, middle class soul.

"Corporate just came down with a directive we have to hire minorities. The guy I was forced to hire has no college and is always late because he didn't have an alarm clock. I bought him a Big Ben and he was still late three out of five times. My hands are tied, I can't get rid of him". I realized immediately I was stranded, since winter ball was over and there were no more paychecks. Though my efforts in the Instructional League had produced an invitation to the major league camp, there was no plan on how to survive between December and February.

My faith was placed in Mary when I called to ask if I could join her family in Elmira. The most logical reason for the request was because her brother, Joe, was serving in Viet Nam and his bedroom was available. Not very romantic, but I had to survive.

"Do you think your mom and dad would mind my coming back and staying in Joe's room"? This came right after Mary said, "Hi". I was in too much trouble to give much of an explanation or give her a chance to say no. She didn't know of my problems with the Army Reserve and their reluctance to grant transfers. Often a request for transfer to another unit caused immediate activation and this something I couldn't afford.

Mary hesitated so long before answering I thought we might have been cut off. But once she collected her thoughts the response gave me chills. "Wait a minute, let me ask daddy". This was being directed to someone who offered one word, "Hello", the first time I came to dinner to meet mom and dad.

Joe Slavin was a dedicated Elmira policeman who enjoyed telling the story about the only time he pulled his weapon. Spotting a burglar going through the rear window of a closed tavern he followed the same route. Nervous about the potential encounter, he made so much noise going through the window the burglar had time to unlock the front door and escape.

Introductions came after pitching a complete game on a hot, humid day. I was riding the high of victory and excited to meet Mary's family. I walked into the house with a six pack of beer, smoking a cigarette, not knowing "Hello" would be the only word offered by Joe over the next two hours.

After a wait far too long for my frayed nerves, Mary returned to the phone. "I can't believe it, but daddy said it was ok. You can sleep in Joe's bed". Even though this is what I wanted, my only response was, "Great, I'll call you tomorrow"! I hung up before there might be any change of heart from either party.

I flew into Elmira after winter ball and the return produced an overall calm feeling. The moment I saw Mary there was a joy hard to describe. I had never been so glad to see someone in my life. Even the transition into her family group was perfect since everyone seemed to be happy for my being there. The anchor had been attached and now I was at a cross roads in life since I would soon leave for Baltimore's major league spring training camp.

NOBODY CAN TAKE AWAY THIS MEMORY

Major league camp was everything a small boy with dreams could imagine. Even though I had come up through the ranks and knew the names, there was a shock when I realized my locker was just a few stalls away from Frank Robinson. It almost matched the meeting with Lefty Grove but this time I was at the same level and could tell Frank "go shit in your hat" and be accepted. THIS is big league status.

A few weeks into camp I was sitting in the lobby of the McAllister Hotel by myself, enjoying who I was and why I was there. The elevator opened and out stepped Frank. "Hey rook, whatcha doing tonight"? Since I was the only "rook", he must be talking to me. "Nothing going on Frank".

My immediate thought for his friendliness was because I pitched batting practice to Robinson his first day in camp, serving perfect medium fastballs up in the strike zone. He nailed six over the fence prompting the Miami-Herald reporter to file a story about how ready Robinson was for the upcoming season based on his timing.

"Motton and Blair are coming down and we're going to a movie. Want to come"? I had played with both in previous seasons and considered them to be friends so the invitation was easy to accept. I answered, "Sure Frank".

What I didn't expect was being led by this Hall of Famer to a sleazy movie theater to see a typical, for the time, scratchy porno movie. Without a doubt, this was the most difficult aspect of spring training to handle besides being demoted. What do you say the next day to the media when their questions are directed toward the obvious.

"How do you feel about your first major league camp and how are the veterans treating you"? My answer would have played out strangely in the Baltimore area if I gave an accurate description of my afternoon with Frank Robinson. "Pitching batting practice to this star was great but we really bonded at the porno theater".

Just being in the major league atmosphere was heady, but since I had taken so long arriving, I wasn't in awe as to talent. What took getting used to was dressing with players who had made it. You wanted to be around when stories were swapped because they didn't talk about Aberdeen, Bluefield or Elmira. Their word pictures were of major cities and classic games that are part of major league history. The best story teller was Boog Powell and my introduction to this jolly giant was a classic.

Boog was a chronic holdout and the press enjoyed this. There were articles written making it sound as if he were a malcontent only interested in money. Reality was, he cooled his heels in Key West during the winter drinking beer and eating large amounts of barbecued ribs. Today, his rib joint beyond the right field fence at Camden Yards is a favorite spot for fans and Powell is often found serving up his favorite food

Word quickly spread. "Boog's here"! Because of his popularity everyone couldn't wait for his arrival. While I was delivering puff balls to the Robinsons, Powell was lumbering across the width of the outfield dressed in a rubber sweat suit. Theory of the day was to melt pounds off in this manner much like wrestlers trying to make a lower weight. There was no concern as to the effect on the body, just run your butt off until you can't go any further.

The clubhouse was empty when I entered the shower but was soon joined by a person twice my body weight. Boog nodded a polite hello but had a quizzical look on his face. We were together ten minutes allowing the hot water to relax our very different muscles. I was the first to leave and went around the corner to groom myself for the night ahead. There was an amazing array of free product and my travel bag was loaded with razors, shaving cream and after shave when I left camp. A classic Yogi Berra quote that applies in describing the quality of major league amenities comes to mind. "The towels were so thick I couldn't close my bag".

Dave McNally had followed me in the practice rotation and was now done and in the shower with Boog. "Hey Mac, who was that kid in the shower, is he a clubhouse boy"? Dave quickly told him I was legitimate and on the roster. My next move was one I couldn't resist after Boog left the shower.

I walked up to Powell and announced, "Boog, before you mistake me for the clubhouse boy, I want to introduce myself". What a sight it must have been. We were both naked and the difference in size meant nothing at this moment. This is one of the beauties of professional baseball. The oddly built person can still make it.

Without warning, he poked his finger in my stomach commanding, "Sit your ass down and tell me all about yourself"! For the next fifteen minutes we talked about my career and not his. When we parted, I felt as if we had played together every season up to this point. Just like pitching to Frank Robinson the first day, I made sure every batting practice pitch to Powell was perfect.

Elrod Hendricks and I ate breakfast together almost every morning in the McAllister coffee shop. He had started his professional career as a catcher in 1959 and bounced all over the map, including four years playing for Jalisco in the Mexican League. Usually this progression downward results in a career ending decision. But somehow Elrod survived and made the Orioles roster the previous year, hitting .202 with 7 home runs. We were now sharing eggs but not prepared in the same manner.

"I'll have mine cracked and served in a cup, if you please". Our waitress responded with, "Do you mean raw"? Elrod nodded his head and I couldn't wait to find out what this was all about. I asked, "Are you sure this is what you want"? My questioning was due to both the freshness of our relationship and because Hendricks was from the Virgin Islands, possibly not understanding eggs normally were cooked in some manner.

"When I was a young boy, I almost died with some kind of stomach problem. You have to understand the power of witch doctor's over our lives. My mother took me to one as a last chance. His advice was for me to drink raw eggs and from that moment on, I improved and was cured. I won't tempt the devil again". When the eggs arrived this morning and every other morning, I tried to watch but couldn't. At the last moment I would raise the morning paper to cover my eyes and would listen to the slurping sound.

Elrod provided assistance in a very delicate matter early in camp since having played with the Orioles the year before, he knew personalities and I didn't. The second time I threw batting practice, the rotation caused Don Buford to step in. His career had started three years prior to mine, but he was a proven major leaguer rising to this level with the Chicago White Sox in 1964. Baltimore had traded to get him for the 1968 season and he arrived with Elrod. To me he was just another batter looking to get his timing from live pitching.

Every pitch I threw was down the middle but Buford wasn't offering to swing at any. After throwing ten down the middle, an attitude set in on my part. Elrod immediately realized the problem and called time out. He came toward the mound picking up stray balls returning them to the cart next to the mound. This was a bit unusual since there were only a few on the ground and I had plenty left in the cart. In his clipped, islander accent he offered, "Hey mon, he doesn't like rookies. Knock him on his ass and let's get on with this".

I followed instructions and delivered a fastball up and in causing Buford to collapse to the ground. My hope was Elrod would give me the standard defense a catcher provides if the batter charges the mound. His job is to come out of the crouch and, hopefully, outrun and tackle the assailant before reaching the pitcher. Since Buford was extremely fast and set a major league record for grounding into a double play the fewest times in major league history, I had to make a decision quickly if he even leaned my way.

Don got up glaring at me without picking up his bat. Elrod was silent and I stood on the mound with a ball in my hand ready for anything. Sensing a shift of control to my side, I put on a happy face which really pissed off Buford. Now he tried to hit everything up the middle with a purpose of hitting me in the head. His swings were over quickly and the next batter stepped in. The next morning at breakfast, Elrod complimented me for my mettle.

Elrod celebrated his 45th year in professional baseball in 2005 by being the Orioles bullpen coach for 37 years. His 28 years at the major league level reached legendary status such as that of Bill Dickey with the Yankees. To have survived so many managerial changes in the Orioles organization and their fall from power tells it all. All new managers want the comfort of choosing their own staff. Hendricks was the glue binding past to the present for a succession of skippers and one of the most loved persons in the game.

Hendricks suffered a minor stroke after a game in Tampa during 2005 spring training and Baltimore announced at the end of the season he would leave the major league coaching staff after the season. His new duties hadn't been determined when he died eight weeks later at the age of 64.

FEW KNOW THIS STORY

A pivotal point in baseball history was reached in 1969 but only a few fans know why. This was the first attempt ever at a player strike, but it was poorly organized, with little publicity, and few believed such a thing was possible.

Marvin Miller, Executive Director of the Major League Players Association had done some math regarding pension money during the contract negotiations and concluded the club's contributions would amount to only $125 per player. Miller put it to a vote and the players could only vote just one way. The count was 491-7 to hold out.

Rookies were asked by each organization if we would cross a picket line to play. My chance to achieve the dream few ever believed could happen, my picture on a collectible baseball card and tailor made uniforms hanging in the locker. Not me, I'm a union man. Are you kidding? I would have swept out the locker room every day if that were a requirement.

Quietly, key players came slipping into camp. McNally had bought a car dealership on a shoe string and Boog now owned a marina in Key West. The best quotes showing the lack of solidarity came in the February 19th edition of the Miami-News written by Jim Huber.

Jim Palmer showed up at the first Baltimore Oriole workout this morning. "I physically couldn't afford to miss any time," said the young pitcher who has been with the club three seasons.

Pete Richert turned out too. "I sure don't want to be here," he said, "I cannot afford to miss a day because of financial reasons. We just bought a house in Baltimore. I can't afford to dip into my funds a day longer. But, I wish I could support the strike by staying out".

The two pitchers, one veteran and one youngster made up one of the largest contingents of name players to show up at any of the major league camps as yet. Others will follow shortly. Their reasons for showing up when the players' union is calling for a strike tends to make the entire boycott threat merely a matter of personal choice.

Jim Huber went on to great success in other media, winning two Georgia Emmy's, six Sportscaster of the Year awards from the Associated Press, five United Press International awards, a Unity Award in Media, two Sigma Delta Chi awards, a Gold award from both the New York and Houston Film Festivals and two Cable ACE's. He also was nominated for a Sports Emmy, the highest award in sports journalism. Another article of his appeared under the most famous picture of my career.

The caption under the photograph across the front sport page read, "One Would Be Oriole Who Knows When To Relax". The subheading read, "Okay, so maybe it is the first day of spring training. And maybe you are a little bit stiff after that cold, cold winter. But gee, Tim Sommers, don't you think you could join in with the rest of the guys? Those might have been the sentiments expressed by his Oriole teammates as Tim Sommers relaxes during exercises at Miami Stadium today. Sommers, a pitching aspirant, didn't join in with his 19 teammates when it came time to "ride their bicycles."

I was in the center of the photo, reclining on the grass while surrounded by six players with legs extended skyward. It looked like the Olympic synchronized swimming team with one out of sync performer in the middle. There was a simple explanation. My back was tender and I felt this was an exercise which could cause a problem the first day of camp.

Weaver was patrolling our circle and I only had to point to my lower back and receive his approval to stop. I remember the feelings at this point perfectly. Temperature in the 70's, bright sunshine, major league status, possible strike breaker, fans in the stands and media coverage. This had been my dream and now I could enjoy the warmth of achievement.

The Miami News was an afternoon paper and after returning to the hotel, I found the sport section lying in the center of my bed. It had been placed there by my roommate but he was nowhere to be seen. I was staring at this embarrassing publicity and knew instantly why it was there. It was a subtle mind game coming from a former number one draft pick by the Orioles who failed miserably in his career but was allowed to keep all of Baltimore's bonus money.

Since the picture was selected by the AP news service, it was transmitted nationally and the personal response was incredible. Friends from around the country cut out their local paper's version and either sent the clipping to me or my parents in Norwalk. I was also featured in a montage of pictures distributed to major companies for their bulletin boards. There I was with the likes of Drysdale, Koufax and Yogi Berra. Unfortunately, there were no captions so the image of loafing lived on.

The February 19th Miami News also summarized baseball's first attempt at a strike with several front page articles. The most defining was that of the beat writer covering the New York Yankees, Al Levine.

Professional baseball was in effect arguing over a few hundred thousand dollars yesterday when Bruce Henry, the Yankees traveling secretary, passed out the $80 checks-a player's two week spring training allowance. John Orsino and Don Nottebart, two veterans with a combined 13 year membership in the Major League Baseball Players Association that is volleying with ownership over pension money, were among the 10 players accepting the checks. Nottebart looked for the signature.

"I'm new here, he said. "Don't know too many names yet." Orsino studied his pay, too, and put it in his locker.

While the majority of the major leaguers stayed home— only pitchers and catchers were to report yesterday—the Yankees came up with two veterans bucking the tide.

Nottebart, a prospective relief pitcher, and Orsino, the former Orioles catcher out to prove his right arm is sound once more, are with the holdouts in spirit, But...."I'm in between this thing." said Nottebart. "Coming back from the minor leagues, I'm a minor leaguer coming to a new club. Reporting was the toughest decision I had to make in baseball. But I couldn't say no."

Much to the expectation of management, six pitchers, four catchers and seven coaches showed up to play catch. "Just when we're trying to get a new image for baseball, said Michael Burke, the Yankee president, "Marvin Miller (the player's negotiator) is trying to make a name for himself," Burke said. "He's in the limelight now. But the players and he are losing perspective of the situation. It's getting out of proportion. Miller's not with the steel workers now. This is baseball."

Orsino and Nottebart aren't with the steel workers; they aren't even with the major leagues. Really, and that's why they're here. "I'm approaching this spring with the realization that this will be my last shot", said Orsino. "I'm 30 years old, not a kid anymore. I just want to make the club. I'd play first base, catch or just warmup pitchers if they want."

Orsino, a six year member of the Player's Association, is trying to make it back to the majors following two arm operations and a comeback season at Savannah in the Class AA Southern League. "Hit about 290-something and the second half of the season my arm was like new."

John first hurt the arm in 1965 in spring training with the Orioles at Miami Stadium. "One throw to second base

152

during infield practice," he said, "I just aggravated it after that." It resulted in bone chips, torn muscle tissue and torn ligaments. He spent the 1966 season on the disabled list and had his first operation. He was traded to Washington, had a second operation the following year and subsequently dropped out of Baseball's Register. "Last year,"

Orsino said, "was the first full year I've played since 1965." John's a non-roster tryout competing with six other catchers, when they all arrive, but he doesn't mind the classification. "All I want is a chance to show somebody I can still play," he said.

Nottebart is a 33 year old, seven year member of the Players Association whose major league. Pitching career goes back to the "Braves" Milwaukee days. He was 5-2 as a reliever at Hawaii last season and thinks that's good enough for the Yanks to give him consideration for a bullpen job.

"I had to weigh three factors before reporting here," Don said yesterday. "I'm not established with this ball club. I'm 33 and this is my first year in the American League. And this club has some fair ball players. I have to try to get in shape, do as good as I can as fast as I can. For me to sit home it would really look good. But I talked to several players and business associates and they said it was better to go."

Nottebart, who has also pitched for Houston and Cincinnati, was a National League dropout on the last day of spring training, 1968, when the Reds wanted to send him to Indianapolis. "It was common knowledge that they wanted me as a safety valve for the younger kids," he said. "I thought I had earned a job and refused to report. I had a 1.94 earned run average the season before. So I was traded to the Chicago White Sox and they sent me to Hawaii. My wife and four kids didn't mind it there."

When Marvin Miller and the owners finally come to terms and the players arrive for spring training, Orsino and Nottebart won't be concerned about grudges.

"They understand my feelings," Orsino said. "If they don't, it's too bad." "Ball players understand each other," said Nottebart. "Anybody who has been to the minor leagues and is trying to get back to the majors will understand."

Late in camp we were notified there would be an important meeting held in the locker room after practice the following day. Negotiations between the player's union and management had concluded and Marvin Miller would be present to describe what gains in the contract had been achieved. Everyone was still in uniform when Marvin arrived and we were gathered in the small, cramped locker room.

"Gentlemen, I'm here to announce the tremendous package we put together for the betterment of professional baseball." His delivery was low key and smooth and didn't sound like a politician blaring about the latest pork barrel bill he had slipped through. Marvin was sincere and the pride he took in his job showed.

Three major gains for players had been made. Up until this point in time, the requirement for a pension was five full years on a major league roster and given the nature of the business, difficult to achieve. Negotiations had reduced the qualifying period to four years due to Satchel Paige. Baseball was extremely worried about the negative press if he ended up on skid row, ignored by the profession who hadn't allowed him to work because of the color of his skin. Also, the age to collect a pension had been dropped from fifty to forty five and there now was a dental plan.

Paige was a legendary black player who reached the major leagues with Cleveland in 1948, the year after Jackie Robinson had broken the color barrier with the Brooklyn Dodgers. This year Satchel was an important element in helping to win the pennant. His record was 6-1 with a 2.47 ERA. The most interesting aspect was his age. Since incomplete records were kept in Mobile, Alabama at the turn of the century for black families, direct descendants of slaves, even Satchel didn't know. Bill Veeck, owner of the Indians hired a private investigator who believed he found a record showing Paige's birth to be 1903. It was difficult to pinpoint since records for the black race were reluctantly recorded.

One of the greatest sport books I ever read was, "Maybe I'll Pitch Forever" by Satchel Page. His commandments for life were even framed by President Eisenhower and hung in the oval office. My favorite was, "Age is a question of mind over matter. If you don't mind, it don't matter". A close second is, "Don't look back, something might be gaining on you".

Next we heard the essence of the agreement and with obvious pride Miller declared, "We now have dental coverage". After covering the plan in detail he asked, "Are there any questions"? Everyone glanced about and the meeting was about to conclude when Earl raised his hand. "Yes Earl, what's your question"? Weaver didn't hesitate. "Are wives covered?" Innocent enough on the surface but loaded with potential humor.

Within seconds, McNally yelled out "Barracuda" and fell back into his locker laughing. You have to understand the person. Dave was very quiet but when he came up with something, it was both accurate and funny. Everyone but Miller knew what he was referring to and like a wave in huge stadiums, laughter moved in a circle around the room. Miller was embarrassed by the activity and waited in the center for an explanation. Earl had turned the color of an overripe beet and had fire in his eyes. Weaver's reputation for being in control was legendary and now had been challenged in a humorous way by McNally.

While Weaver was managing and training in Thomasville, late night cutting sessions were held in "The Bird's Nest". This was a wing only three away from the closest player's residence. If one were brave enough to risk learning of his own fate, crouching below the open windows during these sessions would provide the information. Since there was an unlimited amount of beer available, voices were raised considerably as the night wore on.

Managers and scouts would give evaluations and reasons for acceptance or rejection. This sounds civilized but it wasn't. Weaver's skill was to out shout and intimidate everyone in order to collect the players he wanted. His nickname of "Banty Rooster" was appropriate. He did not back off and by the end of the meetings, everyone had been worn down allowing him to select the best players available for the upcoming season. Your career had been decided under the influence of alcohol, but you weren't invited to the party.

"Barracuda" was the nickname assigned by players to his wife because of a modest overbite and McNally chose that moment to embarrass Weaver. Quickly, Marvin concluded the meeting and left the locker room with the offer to meet with anyone in the parking lot if there were questions. Earl didn't say a word to Dave for the next two days but after that cooling off period, it was business as usual.

This is how Earl managed. He might get in your face one night but it was over soon and, if he felt he was wrong, there would be an apology the next day. His job was to win and if you could help him, you were important and nothing was going to interfere with the goal, not even McNally. Throughout this happening, Frank Robinson sat in his personal double locker grinning.

MY BACHELOR DAYS WERE OVER

When Weaver called me into his office, I knew I was gone since the strike was over and my role of being an insurance policy for the club had expired. But having gone this deep into camp there was personal satisfaction because of my conversation with Walter Youse, Baltimore's most respected scout, at the end of winter ball.

Walter offered, "Tim, you've been invited to the major league camp and there is little doubt you can't make the club next year based on what I've seen." This made a lot of sense to me because of the record I compiled during the last several seasons combined with the dominance in winter ball against the top prospects every organization had to offer.

In this age of baseball there were no sophisticated training facilities as there are now. Earl's office was a small room deep within the stadium and I found him sitting on a chair wearing only a jockstrap, close to the locker of Billy Hunter. Hunter had a mediocre major league career and personified the "good old boy" tag, affording him continuous baseball tenure.

Once I knew it was over I offered, "Well, I met someone in Elmira last year and I think I want to get married, so this will fit in." In retrospect, this was a knee jerk reaction to my disappointment. Earl was great. He had met his second wife while managing in Elmira and understood how easily relationships could occur in this small baseball oriented community. What I was unprepared for was Billy Hunter's response.

"What happened, did you knock her up?" This was delivered with a sarcastic, twisted grin. Quickly I became an observer of Weaver at his best. Earl spun around glaring at Hunter and, without saying a word, put Billy in his place, returning to our conversation.

The manager of the Baltimore Orioles made me feel my future in the big leagues was on the near horizon. I shook Earl's hand while looking at Hunter, who had turned away unable to face me. Surviving that far into the big league process provides a buffer about being demoted. You are going to be only slightly below this level and believe the wait will be short before the call comes.

Once back at the hotel, I reflected on how this skinny kid from Norwalk had reached a position in professional baseball no one believed could happen. Initially there was a raw feeling because of the cut, but soon this was replaced by memories of high school and college friends who did believe in me.

Chuck Russakov, who lent me his fake ID in order to be able drink in California my first season, Roger Parish who, along with Chuck, knew more about my family problems than anyone else, Phil Stall with his quiet intellect, Butch Carpenter who was the quintessential jock at the high school level, Mark Fleisher from Ohio University and the most lovable of all, John Kaiser. I felt I had achieved something that was as important to them as it was to me.

What should have been a direct exit from the room wasn't happening. My bags were packed but my focus was on Elmira and I knew Mary had scheduled a week's vacation to escape the upstate snow. Even though we had been in contact constantly through winter ball, there always was an understanding there was no commitment. I picked up the phone and called. "Well, I got cut but Walter Youse told me again, I should be the first to get moved up."

This statement released something within me similar to the movie, "Manchurian Candidate". Psychological implanting must have occurred. Even though I had expressed the thought of marriage just an hour before to Earl, this memory had been suppressed until Mary and I were talking on the phone.

"I've been thinking about getting married." This was delivered seconds after a benign part of our conversation. I realized immediately what I said and now had to come up with an escape route that would be believable and non threatening to my reputation. "The only way we'll get married is in a Methodist church and with no one around." There was immediate relief now that everything was in the open.

Mary came from a strong Catholic background and I wasn't going to faint in front of strangers at a church wedding. My memory says Mary responded shortly with, "OK". Whether this is accurate is unimportant because my fate had been sealed. "Great! I'll call you from Daytona"! There was no additional conversation, I just hung up.

The door to the room was no more than ten paces away. I moved forward slowly trying to put everything into perspective. Once at the exit I turned and saw my image in a large mirror. I focused on my eyes until this became part of a semi hypnotic trance. I took a deep breath and started speaking out loud to this image.

"Tim, what the hell have you done? Well, you are an honorable person and you wouldn't have said what you did unless you really meant it." Having made this declaration, there was a sense of relief and no turning back. The exclamation point came when I offered a salute to the person in the mirror and said, "I'll see you in Daytona." I walked out the door leaving behind this strange person who had just changed my life.

Because of my travel time, there was the luxury of a day off before officially joining the club. This day was spent meeting with the minister of the Riverside Methodist church, learning his only concern was that Mary and I were of different religions. Mary was Catholic and I wasn't. I explained to the minister why my being Methodist was due to Louie Doud.

Louie was a ninety one year old spinster who owned the home where dad started his insurance business, and we lived within. Her family had been instrumental in the formation of the Norwalk Methodist church and she was the daughter of one of the founders of the AB Chase Piano and Organ Company. AB Chase was a world leader in the music business until the factory burned in the early 1900's. Louie would only rent the upper half of her mansion if this heathen received religious training in her church.

Mary called the night before her flight inquiring as to weather conditions. Daytona was suffering one of the worst cold spells in history and it didn't occur to me she was planning her wardrobe.. There were no sophisticated climatologist graduates doing television and the forecaster assigned to cover shark bites early in the day returned to do the weather. A look out the window of the station would result in, "It's cold out right now, but we'll have sun tomorrow."

What I didn't know was a complete temperature reversal was about to happen. As Mary's flight landed, the temperature was approaching 100 and she stepped off the plane wearing a beautiful wool suit. Our potential marriage was saved only because I had rented a car with air conditioning. "Why didn't you tell me it was going to be so hot?" I still had time to back out and I'm sure at this point, it would have been welcome relief to her. No harm, no foul, just get on with life.

We arrived at the motel with clothing suitable for New York weather. What I hadn't had the nerve to tell her was there was no room reserved for us. Our room was the one assigned to me and another player. He graciously had agreed to bunk elsewhere for the time needed during Mary's stay. During spring break in Daytona there are no extra rooms.

I arranged for blood testing and the church but, naively, wedding rings never entered my mind. I hadn't been to a wedding other than that of my best friend in high school,

Chuck Russakov. I didn't know the best man was required to give a toast. When so informed, I downed enough liquor to produce an endorsement worthy of British royalty.

"We should go to the jewelry store and look at rings because I wasn't sure what you would want". A diamond was out of the question since the only money in my pocket was what I estimated the weeks visit would cost. Mary was nervous and upset with weather shock and just nodded her head in approval.

I quickly reviewed prices and knew what rings were within my range, They were not bargain basement, but not what Mary had in her mind as she flew south. Mary quickly settled into reality by asking me which of the limited choices I liked. The purchase was made and when we walked out I didn't have the nerve to tell her about the advance in pay I had received from our Rochester general manager in order to finance her visit.

The arranged hour at the Riverside Methodist church was two and our small group arrived on time. The Fisher's had agreed to stand up for us since we had been together for three previous seasons and enjoyed each other's company. Tom and Sandy were Catholic and provided moral support to Mary for marrying outside the church. They were from Cleveland and familiar with changes going on within their faith that weren't felt in the small community of Elmira.

We were guided by the minister to a forward portion of the church just beyond the first rows of seats. He stood motionless for a period but there was a smile on his face as he looked at the two of us. The ceremony began and my heart rate increased to the level associated with a long distance run. I heard his words, but they seemed to be directed to that character left behind in the mirror at the McAllister hotel. It was over and we walked up the aisle married, without my having backed out or fainting.

After accepting congratulatory hand shakes I looked back at the minister just before leaving the church. He was still standing with the bible open and the same smile on his face. Some protocol had obviously been missed but I needed help from our friends to save face.

"Tom, should I give him a tip"? To me, this was the only reason our minister could still be standing there, similar to being guided to a seat at a major league stadium by an usher who anticipates a gratuity. Tom gave me direction from this point on in order to avoid embarrassment after having been married for all of five minutes.

"How much money do you have"? All my cash was in the right pocket of my pants with one lone twenty. Tom plucked this bill and returned to the minister. Their conversation lasted so long, it was obvious something was wrong. When Tom finally walked up the aisle he was shaking his head slightly side to side.

"Wasn't that enough?" Since we hadn't paid a penny for anything and caused the minister to do something out of the ordinary, it seemed possible I had under tipped. Tom offered, "I've never seen anything like this ever. He was so impressed by how you presented yourselves about life, he refused money for the service and wishes this to be a wedding present". Tom was a veteran of more than fifty weddings and the sincerity of our minister's statement helped Mary immensely. Even though it was mid afternoon, we slipped away to a quiet spot and hoisted our glasses in appreciation of this endorsement and gift.

Mary went directly to our room when we returned to rest up. To me, it was nothing more than coming back from the park after practice. I went to the small lounge and found half our club watching sports. There wasn't anyone who found my presence to be unusual but there were wives who knew what to do. Within two hours a wedding cake arrived and everyone dined on twenty five cent Crystal Burgers and fries. This celebration was one of the most memorable events of our lives.

My start against the Red Sox club the following day caused my mind to stray from the normal focus. Warming up before a game requires a number of factors most fans don't understand. To me, this is a psychological aspect that isn't understood or taught in pitching instruction to this day. Never in my pro career did I feel better about my upcoming performance. We had been married the day before and the professional high created by the major league camp surrounded me with a cloak of invincibility.

I never got a batter out in the first inning and every pitch was hit with a ferocity that was scary. No matter what I tried, the attack continued. Coming into the game I had the cockiness of a pitcher with credentials that cried out, "How did they keep me from the bigs"! Now, the worry was as to whether I could make the Rochester team. It was only the first inning but these thoughts creep into the psyche quickly.

Rip slowly walked to the mound. My respect for him as a manager and a person had been formed over several seasons. There were fond memories of the baby sitting requests when we had off days and he wanted to take Vi out to dinner. I never refused, and this validated my credentials of babysitting one of the greatest players of all time in Cal, Jr. Cal approached with a grin that didn't match the situation. Everyone was hitting line drives and players were ducking. There were no outs and no time to get somebody ready to replace me. It did not occur to me his trip was missionary in purpose.

"Good God, I have to get you out of here!. You're going to get my whole infield killed!" What he knew, sensed and observed was, my mind was in a place that had nothing to do with baseball at that moment. Rip held his hand out to accept the game ball from me and fans knew this poor soul would never return this spring.

Once I turned the ball over, Rip offered a beautiful declaration. "There's no one back at the motel. Don't even take a shower. I'll see you tomorrow." I remember staring at him waiting for alternative baseball advice. I still wonder what those in the stands thought as I sprinted toward the clubhouse with no reliever in sight. If I were in attendance that day, my thoughts would be the Rochester pitcher leaving the field in such a hurry had an attack of diarrhea.

POSSIBLE GROUNDS FOR DIVORCE

Three days after our marriage I learned of an unusual combination of performers, featuring a live band and a professional hypnotist. I forced Mary to attend even though music didn't interest her and she knew nothing of my interest in all aspects of mental power. Yoga was my choice for a senior term paper requiring considerable research since there were no books in either the Norwalk high school or local library.

My interest in hypnotism came from a most unusual encounter my senior year at Norwalk. The high school had booked a professional hypnotist and I attended the show with my closest friend, Chuck Russakov. What I saw was astonishing. I badgered Chuck until he agreed to join in my search for this wizard. We found him behind the auditorium resting in a small travel trailer. The next hour was fascinating as he taught us a number of memory tricks. If you want to recall something, imagine an elephant with a basket riding on his back. Mentally put the subject inside this basket and pull it out when needed.

He represented, to me, even more mental power than my first psychology professor in college. This person, two years after I left Ohio University, killed his wife, dumping her surgically divided body in a lake near Athens. This was the best lesson for me about intelligence versus logic versus moral responsibility. The metal drum floated to the surface within a short period of time and he was nabbed.

My daughter visited Ohio to feel out whether she wanted to attend this school that held so many memories for me. After her tour started I went to the golf course to occupy the next four hours. I was partnered with the person in charge of the school photo ID card system. Somewhere in the middle of our round I reminisced about my memories of this incident, producing an amazing response. "He was my best friend and just got out of prison two weeks ago. I'm having dinner with him tonight" According to this person, the murder was because his friend learned of an affair between his wife and another faculty member. This ranks high on my lifetime list of coincidental meetings.

The Daytona nightclub held over two hundred people and our table was to the far right of the stage. The band played for an hour before the featured act, Robert Starr, appeared. I was a professional player, we were newly wed and in a major city enjoying the night life.

Starr asked for volunteers and instantly I raised my arm. Mary looked at me and asked, "What are you doing?" She grabbed my left arm, pulling it down to the table while I raised my right arm and became part of the show. Mary wilted and accepted what had happened but it would only get worse for her as the night wore on.

Starr's act was typical in that he selected a group of ten to twelve willing subjects and then narrowed the field. His finale showcased a few of the best and I became the featured act for the night, "Sally the Shape, America's premier strip tease artist. This announcement came after doing many unusual things such as being able to see people naked at their tables. After surveying the audience and registering shock on my face, Robert stuck the microphone in front of me. "What's wrong"? I immediately informed him and the rest in the audience, my wife had no clothes on. This was certainly enough for Mary to wonder what she had entered into.

The main portion of the show was over and we were sent to our seats with nothing apparent as to suggestions given. But I knew I was the star attraction and it was time to prepare. My attire was a sport coat providing a great costume for the featured act. Mary watched as I removed my tie tack at the table and loosened my tie. I was ready to give the best performance of Sally's career. It helped in that I had been sneaking into burlesque shows in Toledo and Cleveland since I was sixteen and knew the routines.

The band started playing "The Stripper" and the spotlight hit me center stage coming close to Tom Cruise's famous entrance in "Risky Business". Even though I can't dance, time spent in burlesque houses gave me all the moves for this moment and I gyrated with a grace Sally would have provided. The tie came off and went between my legs moving slowly back and forth. Next was my shirt. Once this was removed, I twirled it over my head and tossed it backwards, landing on the cymbals of the drummer. The Shape was on a roll.

My tee shirt was next to go but I wasn't about to give it up and further reveal the skinny body with a ball player tan half way up his arms. Also, Sally had a tremendous set of tits and this hesitation wouldn't make sense to her fans. Robert rushed to my side from the shadows.

Whispering into my ear he offered, "Show them your boobies"! This was all that was needed and I proceeded to flash the audience in a provocative manner before removing the tee shirt. The next move was for my pants as this is what the audience was hoping for. Mercifully, Robert came and stopped the act returning my mind to normalcy.

I was confused as to what the powers of hypnosis could produce due to the brief experience in John Maton's bedroom during high school. Our group consisted of John, Phil Stall, Roger Parish and me. John's agile mind had concocted some reasonable explanation to his parents as to why this strange group had been invited to his home.

Since I had the deepest voice and a smattering of knowledge of what to do, I became the instrument, using a candle to provide focus. The suggestion to Phil was he would bend over and untie his shoe when he heard the word "dog". Much to our surprise, he followed the command. Without a word we all went downstairs and said goodnight to John's parents. The power scared all of us to the point nothing was ever said of this night.

Mary returned to Elmira several days later to go back to work and probably sort through what had just happened in her life. Once she left, life was normal as I had known it before, except when I looked at the gold wedding band on my finger and realized there was something different.

THE MIND'S POWER

Mary's departure provided freedom for me to be part of the show nightly. No one on the club knew anything about my activities, even that first night. I was afraid of being labeled as an "intellect" since this could be the kiss of death as far as my career was concerned.

The good old boy network in baseball coaching was mostly an ignorant, rock solid, collection of fraternity brothers passing jobs around. If you went against their grain, you were history. Today, few understand the ramifications of having this label applied. The best illustration of intelligence and the need to keep this element hidden is found in Moe Berg.

Morris "Moe" Berg spent seventeen years in professional baseball as a player and coach and was perhaps the most enigmatic and cerebral figure the game has ever known. At least two biographies have attempted to unravel the mysteries surrounding this American original, described by Casey Stengel as "the strangest fellah who ever put on a uniform". A shadowy figure that had the reputation of appearing and disappearing without warning, Berg was perfectly suited for his espionage work.

After graduating from high school with honors, Berg was accepted at Princeton, an extraordinary achievement at that time for a poor Jewish boy. Berg became a distinguished scholar whose intellectual capacity was boundless. He was a linguistic prodigy, studying seven languages at Princeton, including Sanskrit. He also excelled athletically and was the star shortstop for the school's baseball team. Upon graduating, he continued his education at the Sorbonne in Paris, where he studied linguistics, and later at Columbia University, where he earned a law degree.

Berg played for a succession of major league teams, never experiencing the minors, including the Chicago White Sox, Cleveland Indians, Washington Senators, and Boston Red Sox. Although he was a strong defensive catcher, Moe was slow of foot and a mediocre hitter, with a .243 lifetime batting average and only six career home runs. The stock phrase used to describe his playing abilities was that "he could speak a dozen languages but couldn't hit in any of them." Another quote from Stengel was, "He was as smart a player that ever came along. It was amazing how he got all that knowledge and used them penetrating words, but he never put on too strong. They all thought he was like me, you know, a bit eccentric."

In 1934 Berg was named to an American League all-star team that toured Japan and featured such greats as Babe Ruth, Lou Gehrig, and Jimmie Foxx. Berg was idolized by the Japanese because of his mastery of their language and broad understanding of their culture. Unknowing to his hosts, however, he was secretly filming Tokyo's shipyards, industrial complexes, and military installations from the rooftop of a hospital building. The oft-repeated claim that these images were later used in planning General Jimmy Doolittle's 1942 raids on the Japanese mainland has never been confirmed. After leaving baseball, he joined the Office of Strategic Services, which preceded the CIA as America's first national intelligence agency. Berg would become a highly successful spy during World War II.

Among his many missions on behalf of the OSS was to learn all he could about Adolf Hitler's atomic bomb project. In December of 1944, Berg, posing as a Swiss physics student, attended a lecture in Zurich by Germany's foremost atomic physicist, Werner Heisenberg. Carrying a pistol and a lethal cyanide tablet, Berg was ordered to assassinate Heisenberg on the spot if the scientist suggested a Nazi atomic bomb was imminent. Berg, whose fluent German covered his identity as an American agent, engaged Heisenberg in a casual conversation. The physicist intimated that Germany's nuclear effort was lagging behind that of the Allies. Berg immediately cabled Heisenberg's remarks to OSS headquarters in Washington. President Roosevelt was then debriefed on Berg's report by one of his generals. "Let's pray Heisenberg is right," Roosevelt responded. "And, General, my regards to the catcher." Berg was awarded the Medal of Freedom for his espionage work, but rejected the award "with due respect for the spirit with which it was offered."

Following the war and for the rest of his life, Berg remained an elusive figure. By his own description, he became a "vagabond," living off the generosity of friends. But he always remained faithful to baseball and regularly attended games. A nurse at the Newark New Jersey hospital where he died on May 29, 1972 recalled his final words as, "How did the Mets do today?" He left no estate of any kind and his ashes are buried somewhere on Mount Scopus outside of Jerusalem, but the exact site has been forgotten. In his biography of Berg, "The Catcher Was a Spy", Nicholas Dawidoff wrote that "the final mystery of Moe Berg's inscrutable life is that nobody knows where he is."

After showing up to be part of the show every night for two weeks, Robert greeted me upon an early arrival. "Tim, I want you to consider doing something unusual". Since my mind had been stimulated by this person more than I ever could have imagined, whatever the request, it would be honored. We had worked privately on auto suggestion in order to block distractions when the ultimate focus was required.

"Seldom on the night club circuit do I have a chance to work with someone on an extended basis, who has the mental ability to handle what I would like to do tonight." Even if he had been a lion tamer and wanted to put my head in the lion's mouth, I would have agreed. "Sure, what's it going to be?" Robert hesitated before he continued.

"I want to put you under and place your body between two chairs supporting your neck and ankles. This will be a visual to people in the audience that will illustrate power of the mind that only shows up in newspapers when the headline reads, "Woman Lifts Car Off Child" I weighed 152 and he weighed 175. "Let's do it!"

Once the show was over, with an inferior Sally performing, Starr made a special announcement that kept people in their seats. "Ladies and gentlemen, you have the opportunity to witness an unusual event." He proceeded to explain our relationship, giving validity for what was about to happen. "You will observe first hand the unlimited power of the mind over the body." Those in the audience who were moving toward the exits stopped and returned to their seats.

With total silence in the club, Robert started counting down from ten suggesting my body was becoming as rigid as a bar of iron. The count was slow but the constant reinforcement as to what was happening produced the most amazing effect. There was a power never felt before, and as we progressed my body became that bar of iron. Two members from the band grasped each arm and tried to pull them away from my body but couldn't. After the show, Robert told me this was the indicator as to whether he should continue.

I was tilted like a slab of cement and placed between two chairs with support on my neck and ankles. Since my eyes were closed, there was no anticipation as to what was next. Starr placed a foot in the middle of my stomach and applied pressure. I sagged but immediately returned to a perfectly rigid horizontal posture and then his entire weight was upon me. This lasted for twenty seconds, but enough time for the audience to become alive and an ovation spread around the room. They had witnessed exactly what he had promised and would leave with a better understanding of their own power.

We had talked extensively in our down time about his involvement with other sports. What he was doing then is now in vogue, but totally unheard of at this point in time. He was a sport psychologist with marketable skills but bouncing around the night club circuit before the lucrative profession was invented. What I wanted was the ability to perform perfectly during the ninth inning of the seventh game of the World Series. This picture would be bases loaded, two men out, three and two count on the best hitter of the opposing club. Snap off the perfect curve and I'm being considered for Cooperstown.

OUR MARRIAGE WAS NOT TYPICAL

Mary's return to Elmira left me in shock. Best of all worlds were there for me since I was married, alone, and in Daytona Beach during Easter break. The memory of the impromptu reception put together by the wives of the Rochester team was all I had, but fading.

We were back talking on the phone just like before, but changes had occurred in my life. I was a professional ballplayer and something was different. Complex ingredients had been put together and much like a fine wine, needed time to mature.

Mary had transferred to Rochester Telephone and our one room apartment was near the inner city. Now that we had moved to a metropolitan area the rents were considerably different and this was all we could afford. It didn't matter we couldn't get to the bathroom unless the bed was folded back into the couch.

Twenty years later we brought Chris and Jeff to our marriage starting point and because the apartment was empty, all had a chance to peer in through the windows. There was shock as to the size, but also a flashback to the night we were on our sleeper sofa listening to a Red Wings game. WHAM radio was blessed with a broadcaster by the name of Joe Cullinane. Joe came from an era that produced another person with the ability to produce great, believable recreations of a sporting event on radio. His name was Ronald Reagan.

A Western Union ticker tape was fed to the station by someone at the park with a time delay in the information flow that was minimal. The skill in reporting was to maintain the game atmosphere and if you listened closely, one could hear the recorded loop of crowd noise including the same vendor selling his wares. The most convincing illusion to authenticity was the crack of the bat. Culinane and Reagan used the same device, a stationary block of wood much like that of a butcher block and something resembling a gavel.

My Army Reserve commitment this night caused me to remain in Rochester while the club was on the road in Toledo. Mary and I snuggled up, tuning in to hear Joe's broadcast and how well our team would do without me. The ticker only provided Joe with details such as ball one, strike one, base hit, etc. His skills were his imagination and knowledge of our team. While there were abrasive reporters in the clubhouse demanding information all the time, Joe was so low key you felt he was on the roster. Many inside clubhouse details were his alone.

"Beene's in trouble and despite a big lead, there's activity in the bullpen. Ripken can't let this game get away. Let's put the binoculars on the pen and see who's warming up. Well, it's Sommer. He just came off a good outing and is the obvious choice". This was going to be good and maybe my record and ERA were going to get better while we listened in our folding bed.

Fred had the best record this year, 15-7 with a 2.98 ERA and was riding the Weaver wave forward. The irony was the reversal in our careers. Fred's record in Appleton during the 1964 season was 11-5 with a 2.22 ERA. He jumped to Elmira the following year at the AA level while I was back proving myself in Kennewick. He was exempt from military duty because of his married status and I wasn't. Cullinane had no idea as to my staying behind because of military obligations.

"A sharp single to right by Conigliaro drives in another run. Rip has to make a change, Beene's tiring". Since there was a lag of about one minute, Joe had to sweat out the moment. When his ticker announced another pitcher, he had to retreat from his firm commitment to me and have something believable to the listeners. "Something happened to Sommer in the bullpen and Cal has brought in Severinson without any warm up". Since I wasn't in the game, I gave Mary a kiss goodnight and turned out the lights.

On our second day, after settling the household, there was a rain out early and a chance to do something in a city offering far more cultural choices than Elmira. Mary couldn't know how important these unscheduled off days were and what the Mathias brothers did to create one in Appleton during the 1964 season.

There had been rain the night before, but not enough to cancel the game. Our crew of five arrived at the ball park around eleven in the morning. Three of us kept Ralph Mueller tied up with questions mostly related to our contracts while the brothers Mathias hooked up a garden hose, flooding home plate and pitching mound.

The questioning continued for another half hour knowing some water had to be absorbed. Finally I suggested, "Let's go look at the field". The infield was still damp but repairable with a lot of work before game time. But the two areas attacked by John and Bobby were more than our limited ground crew could handle.

After viewing the scene Mueller declared, "I don't understand, the field normally drains well in these areas. There's no way to do everything in time, we'll just have to call the game". We gave an Academy Award performance expressing our desire to play but understanding his looking out for our safety. When the rest of the team learned of the cancellation we were heroes for a day and it was party time in Appleton.

Mary was exhausted. I can't remember whether we had dinner when the announcement came on the Rochester radio station, tickets were still available for the second performance by Janis Joplin at the Eastman Theater in the center of the city. I subjected my new wife to torture by demanding we attend this concert. I believed Janis possessed the greatest female voice in the history of rock and roll and Mary could care less.

Eastman was a gift from George Eastman, founder of Kodak, opening in 1922, having cost $6,700,000 to construct. The designer, Lawrence White, also had Penn Station in his portfolio. High above there was a chandelier fourteen feet in diameter, thirty five feet tall and weighing five thousand pounds. Somehow this magnificent piece did not drop during Joplin's performance.

The lobby was holding the crowd for the second show which was running a half hour late. There were three hundred people jammed into the lobby and pot smoke was so thick there was no way you couldn't have a buzz going. Characters in costume were all about and fascinating. This was the end of the flower child era, but a large group had come to hear Janis without knowing when this star would flame out. Within the next year Janis, along with two other legends, Jimmy Hendrix and Jim Morrison, would leave this earth.

The first audience went out side doors and we were able to reach our seats quickly. The Eastman main floor seated several thousand with a beautiful balcony above. We had been able to get prime center seats and I couldn't wait for the lead band to conclude. They were a marginal group who had one song familiar to most but their sole purpose was to build excitement.

Janis came running out the same time "The Kozmic Blues" did. Her band usually came to their instruments and then set a tempo for the diva's entrance, but not this time. She was swigging heavily from a bottle of Southern Comfort and took a seat on the right front of the stage accepting the touch of fans as they came forward.

Janis's feelings about performing were, "When I sing, I feel like when you're first in love. It's more than sex. It's that point two people can get to what they call love, when you really touch someone for the first time, but it's gigantic, multiplied by the whole audience, I feel chills. The more you live, the less you die".

This show was the most dynamic of all concerts I ever attended because of her raw emotion. Since her performance had affected me, I turned to see Mary's reaction but she was asleep. Her appearance wasn't unusual since the majority of the audience were in the same state given the time of night and drugs ingested. I jammed for two hours alone.

Soon my brief modeling career started in Rochester. Under the terms of the contract we were required to appear at a moments notice for anything. No extra money, just be there or face a fine. This type of control makes it easier to understand some of the underpinnings surrounding creation of free agency and a power shift to players.

McCurdy's was the elite department store in center town Rochester and this is where we were told to go. There was a Father's Day promotion and we were the premier event to kick off everything. There was no consideration as to individual or family plans needing to be changed on short notice, just be there or else.

It was now show time and twenty five players were awkwardly moving about back stage after being assigned clothing by the young female coordinator. She was direct from New York City and handled major showings for well known designers. Clothing was randomly assigned and, fortunately, I wasn't asked to don a bathing suit. Next were instructions on how to walk an elevated runway for thirty feet doing turning movements when reaching the end. Mary was somewhere in the audience hiding along the fringes of the room. Just like my stripper act in Daytona, the coordinator had saved me for last

I had been given a pair of designer slacks that were so tight nothing was left to the imagination and my shirt was color coordinated and sheer. Even though I was nervous it was now time to perform. The curtain parted and my walk started in sync with the fashion coordinator's description as to what was being worn. Half way down the runway catcalls and whistles started. It was the hip action that had developed because of the injuries suffered during the 1964 season. To eliminate pain, my body had adopted a pronounced swivel as I walked.

The first time this action became known to me was while window shopping mid afternoon in Providence, Rhode Island. Someone tapped me on the shoulder and upon turning a very attractive girl offered, "I love the way you walk"! After mumbling "Thanks" I practically ran away leaving her standing alone on the sidewalk. After all, what kind of girl would say such a thing to a guy?

I was really enjoying this attention from so many females and during the return I took my time adding just a little more movement to the hips. This is what being a professional is about. The crowd didn't know there had been a subtle adjustment to provide better entertainment value. This was great and I resisted the temptation to make another trip down the runway. Instead, I merely took a bow and headed off stage left. The Rochester Democrat Chronicle did a feature story the following day about the show and my review came at the end of the article.

"The star of the show was Tim Sommer, a relief pitcher for the Red Wings. His thin build lent itself perfectly for the tailored Da Vinci slacks. However, he modestly kept on his undershirt beneath the diaphanous shirt made by Kreeger. The audience applauded his style walking the runway as he appeared to be the most accomplished of the players doing this sort of thing." If only I had an agent.

TRYING TO CLIMB THE MOUNTAIN

Even though I had been converted to short relief in 1967, one of my best games came as a spot starter the following year. Most always, the spot starter was a middle reliever geared to coming in early and going as far as possible. Cal Ripken appeared in front of my locker minutes after I walked into the clubhouse and because of the grin on his face, I knew what was up. "You're on the hill." The assignment was accepted without question.

Pittsfield was producing a typical hot, humid Sunday afternoon at an old historic park in the heart of the Berkshire Mountains. Most pitchers dreaded playing at Wahconah Park because of the irregularity of the fence distances. The left field line was deep but right field was as short as Yankee Stadium and a creek ran behind the park, dictating fence positions. The park is unusual in that batters face west, meaning late in the day the setting sun was in every batters eyes. The park was also known for the artificial owls that hung in the rafters to keep birds from nesting in the rafters above fans.

The first baseball game on this site took place in August, 1892 and Wahconah, the current stadium, was built in 1909 and is registered with the National Register of Historic Places. An ambitious effort is under way, led by Jim Bouton, to raise $4 million dollars for renovations.

The game was not long in duration because I never wasted time between pitches or innings. Since there were no muscles requiring elongation, only three or four warm up throws were required before others were ready. My record still stands in the Midwest League for the fastest nine inning game, played in one hour and thirty minutes. The record goes to the winning pitcher. My teammates were excited since we were out on the town early.

The opposing Pittsfield pitchers were matching me inning by inning. Cal Ripken declared this was the best game, overall, he had seen in either his playing or managing career. Every professional aspect came into play, including managerial decisions which weren't normal.

The sun had set to a point affecting each batter and had to be factored by pitcher and catcher since both had to be in sync as to pitch location. To me, it was the closest I would come to understanding what it takes for a professional boxer to receive continuous punishment and still continue. Each inning I had to will myself to walk across the lines once again.

Rip removed me in the thirteenth inning with the score tied at 1-1. I had fifteen strikeouts, one shy of my professional high of sixteen against Davenport four years prior. Three thousand fans rose to their feet, giving me the greatest ovation I was ever to receive. It was a statement as to the quality of effort by both sides and the only time I walked off the field with everyone standing. The scorecard as to future major league players from this game reads, Pittsfield-15, Elmira-7.

I wanted to shower and watch the finale but my body shut down. Alone, I almost passed out in the clubhouse because of dehydration and had to lie on a hard bench to stabilize. If any help was needed I was out of luck since my body wouldn't be found until after the game. There were no ambulances at the park and the nearest medical facility was five miles away.

After recovering, I walked up the ramp during the fifteenth inning just in time to witness the game winning home run for Pittsfield given up by our best relief pitcher. The stands emptied and I was alone with my thoughts for thirty minutes before our bus returned to the hotel. This was the point in my career to decide whether I should commit more time trying, or step away and get on with life.

This game told me I had the ability to make it. Four years of starting was solid, conversion to short relief was successful and this game reinforced my belief there wasn't a role I couldn't handle. Since a report was required after each game, Cal's words to me had to be on an evaluation forwarded to Baltimore. There was to be reinforcement when I was called up to Rochester later in the year.

The Red Wings were closing in on the league lead under the management of Billy Demars and his bullpen needed help. Billy had benefited from the two best years of my career supporting his winning league championships. At this point, he didn't have to out shout Weaver to get who he wanted.

When I joined the team, there was a noticeable shift as to intensity of being in a pennant race at this level. Lower leagues produce a feeling of doubt because of little player experience for reference. During the season, the Rochester roster had twenty-four players that had played in the major leagues or would get there. A level of confidence spread over everyone from the front office to club house attendants.

An adjustment had to be made on my part because of increased media coverage. There were few reporters seen within club houses at lower levels asking for quotes from either players or manager. Now, I was being asked to speak on the record for newspaper, radio and television. Few interviews were used because of my fear of overstepping rookie boundaries during a pennant race.

There had been no warning this night as to what was ahead as I finished dressing. If team bonding happens at this point of the season, a pennant is within reach. You become closer to your teammates than your wife and if there isn't a partnership with a woman who understands this, there will be trouble in the relationship.

My uniform had been tailored to match my thin build and I had the look of a potential major league player deserving to play at this level. The last piece of equipment was my Red Wing hat sitting perfectly centered at eye level on the shelf. I could smell the unique sausages called, "white hots", being grilled just outside the club house. There was plenty of time to have one before strolling to the bullpen, signing autograph requests along the way. A speed bump to this plan appeared when the hat was lifted and a pristine white baseball was underneath.

Only someone who had played the game for awhile would know what had happened. I was going to be starting within the next hour against Richmond who, this year, had the third highest total of home runs out of eight teams, led by Dave Nicholson with 34. An irony is, Nicholson was a former Baltimore farm hand playing for Aberdeen in 1959 and managed by Earl Weaver. He had career numbers with 35 home runs and 114 RBI and was part of a wild group that included Bo Belinsky and Steve Dalkowski.

Leaning to the left slightly, I could see into the manager's office. Billy was watching and waiting for a reaction. No one else, outside of whoever came up lame this night, knew what he had done. Without saying a word to either Billy or those remaining in the club house, I left for the bullpen without my white hot.

There was no change in my demeanor as I stopped along the way to accommodate autograph requests, but emotions were hard to harness. At the end of a pennant drive, Billy had given me the opportunity to prove myself, once again, to the organization. The bullpen catcher this night was Vic Roznovsky and he was already in the pen when I arrived.

Vic was someone who had bounced around the bigs with limited success and we barely knew each other from spring training this year. He had not developed the elitist attitude because of his having been in "the show" and you hadn't. He was a nice person and could care less about class separation. Even though less than fifteen minutes remained before the start of the game, he was ready. Roznovsky was in full gear when I gave him the game ball I found beneath my hat. Being the veteran he was, there was an understanding and just asked, "Do you have enough time?" The answer to the question was there five minutes later when I walked to the mound.

My two hundred plus professional games produced different expectations each time. There were moments in the bullpen when everything was perfect but failed to carry across the lines for some unknown reason. There was a game in Kennewick when I was so ill with the flu, Cal Ripken had to wake me in the club house to start the game. My "stuff" was poor but I outwitted the opposition, pitching a complete game while sweating out the virus.

This game was just another unknown, but there was a difference. What Billy had done was "old school" and an accepted practice since no player had the option of refusal. He didn't want to give me time to think about what was ahead but, more importantly, he could have been crucified by the press if I failed.

My catcher was Del Bates and there was no connection between the two of us prior to this night. Bates had started within the Orioles organization at Tri-Cities two years prior to my turn there, but due to shifting and trading he didn't come back to the organization until this year. His only taste of the majors was the next year with Philadelphia, hitting .133, with 1 home run.

Since Vic did the short warm up, Del had to adapt quickly to what I wanted to throw. Had Demars been conventional, there would have been a quick meeting in the clubhouse between the three of us. My catcher received the typical four tosses that couldn't give him any feel as to how to call the game. Bates proved to be a quick read and a master game strategist. What helped was my control of pitches, giving him confidence in calling for something to upset the thought process of a hitter. He and I were locked into a unique understanding that usually only develops over a full season.

Billy removed me late in the game without either side having scored. The lead off batter in our bottom of the inning was Merv Rettenmund. Merv hit a monstrous home run to left center for the only run of the game with Paul Knetchges and Al Severinson closing the deal. Demars had gambled and I was the winner.

Merv went on to win the International League Player of the Year award. He hit .331 with 22 home runs and it seemed perfect we had joined for this game since our first connection came during the ill fated season with Stockton. He possessed trivia potential from the aspect of being drafted by the Dallas Cowboys out of Ball State. His stride and speed were that of a classic sprinter, thrilling me more than any other player, except for Lloyd Fourroux, going for an extra base hit as there was an overdrive few had.

Rettendmund's actual home run swing had been captured by a photographer and was featured across the front page of the Chronicle sport section. My coverage was, "The thin, bespectacled right hander, recently called up from Elmira, pitched seven strong innings before Ripken turned the game over to the bullpen". Instead of buying out the news stand, I bought one paper.

After a win there was no sleep as my mind wouldn't allow release from the high nor did I want it to end. All night long I could see every pitch as if there were a center field camera replaying the scene. This was the positive reinforcement needed to carry over to the next game.

Billy called me into his office the next day and started the conversation with another, "I just talked to the front office". Having heard this too many times before and the way it was delivered told me my bags needed to be packed. "Baltimore just activated Gatewood". It was obvious Demars had been placed in a non negotiable position by the Orioles.

Aubrey Gatewood's contract had been purchased from Tacoma where his record was 1-1 with a 4.62 ERA. His twelve year major league career would finish at 70-69 with only two winning seasons along the way. There were three unsuccessful seasons with the California Angels from 1963-65 and now he was going to be dressing in my locker.

Because there is so little minor league information available it becomes hard to analyze statistics or find articles about any player. I was able to find a thread tying Gatewood to the Orioles organization. The 1962 Kennewick club wasn't part of Baltimore's system, but there was one member of their pitching staff out on loan, Paul Knechtges. He had been optioned to another organization this season but must have provided a reference for Gatewood. Aubrey's stats for the Atoms were 1-2 and a 9.96 ERA.

Gatewood was now playing for Rochester and Billy was saddled with a pitcher who finished 4-10. Rochester lost the pennant by five games and I had thrown a shutout before being replaced.

BASEBALL'S STAR HAD FLAWS

It isn't often when a vortex is formed pulling two major league teams and one minor league team into the same center, but the phenomena surfaced in Daytona Beach in 1969. The Yankees and Dodgers were on their swing north after breaking camp and we were away playing the Boston AAA club in Deland.

Our bus on the return had a hard time finding a parking spot since all three clubs were trying to do the same and there was little room in the lot. This wasn't a screw up by the major league teams because, without their knowing, the visitor's clubhouse had been condemned recently due to unsanitary conditions.

Island Park was old and now there were almost one hundred people jammed into the interior of a cement block structure more fitting for a small town Texas high school football program. I had finished our game with the Red Sox returning to the club house tired and sweaty.

"Who's Sommer"? Maury Wills wanted to know. Since my locker was next to both the soda machine and the front door, I negotiated an agreement with this Hall of Famer with a free Coke for me, and a discussion about baseball with him. Wills was just as interested in knowing who I was as Boog Powell had been before. Maury showed me prototype shoes Wilson had developed for him that were ultimately outlawed because they closely resembled track shoes with pointed spikes.

Seven lockers away sat the one player I wanted to meet more than any other, Mickey Mantle. There were three front office people in suits guarding his small space providing privacy. Even though we were all enjoying this strange union of teams, Mickey wasn't allowed to participate even if he wanted to. This was the first year after his retirement and he was in camp for the sole purpose of publicity. Since I was part of the inner sanctum there was time to experience the feel of being in the big leagues and observe this faded star. Mantle had batted only .237 his final season, the worst of his career.

Once Wills had dressed and was moving around, I had a chance to lean back into the shadows of my locker and watch Mickey. He had put on his uniform quickly, sitting motionless and staring at his hands. The body language told me he didn't want to be there at all. I was most surprised by his youthful look and muscular build that wasn't hidden by the uniform. Since I couldn't get to him, it was now time to circulate and press the flesh.

There were so many people in the small clubhouse it was hard to move about. Finally, I entered the trainer's room and couldn't believe my eyes. Getting a rubdown was one of my boyhood idols, Jim Bunning. He was both idolized and hated since his best years were for Detroit, always defeating Cleveland. I didn't hesitate a second before offering my hand and introducing myself. This is the essence of being a professional athlete. We were in the same fraternity where friendship is welcomed and encouraged. Lefty Grove taught me this lesson my first day under contract in his living room.

"Jim, did you ever hurt your back in your career?" "Yeah I did, why do you ask?" I went on to tell about my experience in Dubuque and wondered if his pitching style had changed like mine. Bunning was notorious for falling off toward first base side after a pitch and losing his cap. What is important about this motion is the inability to field one's position to the right, needing the third baseman to move in closer than normal. This was a flaw in my game and I was curious.

"That's the problem I've had since hurting my back along the away and the reason I'm getting my rub down now. If a bunt goes down third, I hope my third baseman can get to it or goes foul". There were a few others to greet before time to take a shower and watch the game. My ten minutes with Bunning were priceless but provided no clue he would become one of America's most respected Senators.

Just as my wool inner sweatshirt was above my head, I was slapped in the stomach with enough force to surprise and hurt. I yanked it off and looked up at someone I didn't know at all. He had a big grin on his face and an extended right hand. "Hi, I'm Steve Hamilton and I've been looking to meet you for a long time"! Since there was no response on my part, he continued. "Yep, I've been trying to find someone in pro ball skinnier than me and now I've found him".

Hamilton also played with the NBA's Minneapolis Lakers, becoming one of only two professional athletes to play in both a Word Series and a NBA championship series. He saved the sixth game of the 1964 World Series and in 1965 recorded a 1.39 ERA in 46 games. Steve went on to serve eleven years at his alma mater, Morehead State, as athletic director and during his tenure, he saw graduation rates of the Eagle athletes improve and MSU win the Ohio Valley Conference's academic achievement award four times. With our bonding because of physical similarities, he was most curious as to the obstacles I had to hurdle and I was glad to fill him in.

Our 1969 Elmira club had the opportunity to tap into a resource none of us ever expected. This was the year of the hybrid team combining several organizations with a manager no one knew, Harry Bright. There were eleven players who eventually got their baseball card issued, but we finished 20 games out of first. Two pitchers, Mike Corkins and Rick James combined for 12 wins and 25 losses, but went on to the bigs later. They weren't in the Orioles organization but Lloyd Fourroux and I were and though we had winning records, we were stuck in Baltimore quicksand.

189

Bright started his career in 1948 with Twin Falls in the Pioneer League and recorded his last active game in 1971 with Burlington in the Midwest League. In between he was on the roster of 26 professional teams but the one most important to us was the New York Yankees. He became our Jim Bouton, providing amazing inside stories about America's most admired team. The best story telling came one night on the road and he took his time describing the scene.

Harry's first year with the Bronx Bombers was 1963 and his only notable accomplishment was to become Sandy Koufax's 15th strikeout victim in game one of the World Series, then a WS record. His first road trip was to play the Angels and experience the west coast atmosphere, playing for a winner. The prior year, he hit a career high 17 home runs for a last place Washington club while Mantle hit 30 for the pennant winning Yankees. This season he was third string behind Elston Howard and Johnny Blanchard, happy to be with a pennant winner and not with last place Washington who would lose 106 games.

When the Yankees checked into their hotel, everyone's mailbox had an invitation to attend a lavish party at a famous movie director's mansion in the Hollywood hills Sunday after the game. According to Harry, the two day build up caused many to lose focus, producing conversation not only in the club house but on the bench.

Limousines picked up the majority of the club at the hotel and each limo had a bartender to mix drinks on the way. Upon arriving, players were greeted on the front lawn by the most beautiful women LA had to offer. It turned out they were a curious mixture of aspiring actresses and the city's best prostitutes with not much distinction between the two. The director knew how to make everyone feel welcome.

The party morphed into a movie scene because of the surroundings. There were beautiful and famous people everywhere. Each player was going to enjoy one of the most pleasurable nights of his life with no expense, no worry and, most importantly, no publicity. This idyllic setting ended with a slap and a scream.

There were no women of color at the party and when a black player proposed retiring to one of the mansion's many bedrooms, a crisis developed. The problem might have been solved if this request hadn't happened next to the host. "What do you mean you won't go to bed with him? I guarantee you will never work in another picture for me or anybody else in this town"! After the threat, he delivered an open handed slap to her face for emphasis.

Harry told us a chill was thrown on the mood of the party and everything shut down. The player was extremely embarrassed and the rest of the club could see a tabloid headline developing. Harry never revealed the director's name or player, so I can't list whether either won an award during their respective careers.

Bright also offered insight as to the problems Mantle had with alcohol. Baseball wasn't that far removed from the days of train travel and regular reporters traveled with their teams, also drinking with them. What they observed never saw print, especially if it involved Mantle. According to Harry, many checks had to be written to pay for damages when Mickey got out of control.

Babe Ruth was larger than life and reporters reveled in telling tales about his gargantuan excesses because he welcomed stories enhancing his reputation, both on and off the field. The difference was in the personalities. Ruth embraced life with a smile and Mantle was forever angry with the cards dealt to him.

At age nineteen he left the lead mines of Oklahoma for professional baseball and the strongest influence on his life at this point was his father, Mutt Mantle. Mutt's grip on Mickey was so strong that Mantle married his wife, Merlyn, because his dad told him so. Mantle was a switch hitter because his father knew it would give his son a greater chance to play when he reached the majors.

Mickey was resigned to the fact he would live a short life because Mutt died of the family disease, Hodgkin's, at age 39. He turned to alcohol because he didn't think he'd live past 40. His grandfather and two of his uncles also succumbed to the same disease before their 40th birthdays. The knee problems that plagued his career were at least in part of a prolonged function of his drinking. A quote from a book written, by Tony Casto, "Mickey Mantle: America's Prodigal Son" says it all and provides substance to Harry's stories.

"There is no doubt in my mind that alcohol hurt my career terribly. In the end, all you really have are the memories and the numbers on paper. The numbers are important because baseball is built on them, and this is the way you are measured. And the point is, I played in more than 2400 games, more than any Yankee player in history, and I hit 536 home runs, and I shouldn't be griping about my career. But I know it should have been so much better, and the big reason it wasn't is the lifestyle I chose, the late nights and too many empty glasses". Late in life before liver cancer ended his party, Mickey offered, "If I knew I was going to live this long, I would have taken better care of myself."

Bright was among an afternoon gathering in the lobby of our York, Pa hotel when a broadcast of the Little League World Series came on. The intro was lengthy since the buildup featured a history of the color commentator, Mickey Mantle. The feature was over and network went to a commercial. Harry said to no one in particular, "I'll bet my paycheck the son of a bitch is drunk". It didn't take long after returning to air before Harry's prediction came true. After a two minute lead in by the prime reporter, commentary was turned over to Mantle.

The first words from Mickey were terribly slurred in a long rambling speech that dissolved into total mush. Nothing he said made any sense. The network hit the kill switch on his microphone and several minutes of action went unreported. Once there was a resumption Mantle was gone from the scene for more than ten minutes. His return to the airwaves was limited to basic "yes" and "no" responses. Bright sat in his seat not with an "I told you so" look, but one of sadness as his memories about Mickey had surfaced amongst a group so young, most of their knowledge of this person came from the back of Mantle's baseball cards.

NOBODY KNOWS THESE LEGENDS

The worst thing in professional baseball is the unrecorded histories of all who didn't reach the major league level. Lost are stories going back to an era before a minimum salary of $500 per month had been established and blacks were denied access to professional baseball. This encompasses legendary people who will only be remembered by a diminishing base similar to that of survivors of America's wars, whose memories are lost forever. I signed a contract only fifteen years after Jackie Robinson had broken the color barrier and minor league players of his era typically made entry level salaries of $150 or less each month, but only because they were white.

I had the privilege of playing with three of these characters. One is legendary within baseball's inner circles and the others are only slightly less recognized. But all have reputations spawning stories that, to some, are unbelievable. Baseball at this time teetered on the edge as a game played for fun versus the grab for money and soon went the wrong way.

HARD AS A ROCK

As if my nerves weren't bad enough about making a team my first camp, a strange group arrived during an afternoon lunch providing more pressure. Twenty plus players were ushered into our cafeteria and treated like royalty. Word spread quickly they were the Wake Forest baseball team on a southern swing and would be playing the next day against one of our four groups. This produced an understanding for how large my pond had grown and the bigger fish I had to battle for survival.

The most intriguing member of the team was out of perspective with the rest. The shortest, stockiest, best dressed, baldest person was Billy Scripture and I could identify with this person who didn't fit the norm. Billy was to become an All American at Wake and has been inducted into their Sport Hall of Fame.

This status was achieved even though he was almost expelled for practicing his batting stroke by chopping down beautiful old trees in the woods next to the football stadium. A negotiated settlement resulted in having Scripture chopping the felled trees into firewood and delivering the logs personally to professor's homes on campus. Little did I know Baltimore would draft him and we would play together for five seasons. What comes to mind is Billy's unbelievable grasp as to the subtle nuances for the game.

He was one of the first instructors hired by Ewing Kauffman (owner of the Kansas City Royals) to staff his inventive idea for a baseball academy. The theory was to combine continuing education with intense daily baseball instruction within a college campus atmosphere. College level courses were provided along with a skilled baseball staff. Study in the morning and play in the afternoon. The plan failed after a few years with several million dollars of

Kauffman's money having been spent. The only graduate to reach the majors was Frank White with the Royals.

Scripture's skills carried over to his being hired to manage in the minor leagues at various levels, but his many quirks got in the way of success. One night in 1984 I was swinging around the channels and caught a lead in to David Letterman's show. "Tonight, ladies and gentlemen we'll have as our guest one of the legends of baseball."

Billy had his fifteen minutes of fame and it was fascinating. Letterman asked him if it was true that, after having been kicked out of a game, he had climbed the light towers and managed the game from high above, flashing signals as if he were standing in the third base coaches box. Scripture's answer was "yes." The opposing manager objected to the legality and after a long delay and consultation with the general manager of the club, it was determined the light towers were not part of the umpires jurisdiction. This story pales by comparison to my memories of this unique character.

Early on Billy became infamous for being impervious to pain. My former roommate, Don Baylor, set a major league record for being hit by a pitch and if Billy had made "the show", he would have given Baylor a run for that title. Both had the physique, mentality and reflexes allowing a quick turn, head tuck, and trot to first. Billy took this absence of pain to a different level producing a reputation that had to be seen to be believed.

Every year Scripture would allow the latest hard throwing draftee to settle in with his cockiness well in place. Since Billy was always available for multiple duties, he occasionally would serve as a bullpen catcher. The greater the ego the better, especially if a large signing bonus was involved. At some point during the warm up he would simply throw the catcher's mitt to one side and remain in position. The pitcher would stop the process and wait for Billy to retrieve the mitt. Scripture's only move was to hold up his right hand and offer, "You don't have shit on the ball tonight and I'll catch whatever you want to bring with no glove"!

The shock value was classic. Like a cartoon bull with smoke coming from both nostrils, the bonus baby would let loose with his best heat. Billy snatched it out of the air deftly and without a grimace. Being a master at this and not wanting to repeat the challenge, he would walk the ball up to the demoralized bonus baby, returning to the dugout without another word said.

An enduring memory of Billy is his taking infield practice without a glove. Scripture's reputation was so great that if he decided to perform on a particular night, the opposing club would come back to the dugout rather than relaxing in the clubhouse. Our coach launched ground balls with a thinly shaped instrument called a fungo. He knew what Scripture wanted and hit the ball as hard as he could, producing drives harder than most balls during a game.

Billy would drop to his knees, blocking the ball with his chest and casually throw to first base in a manner that would have resulted in an out every time. This was repeated until he knew a psychological imprint on the opposition had been established. Few knew this was not an act. It was part of Scripture's meticulous preparation because this might happen during the course of the game and he wanted to be prepared.

Scripture's teeth were also legendary. My lament is that I didn't ask him for x-rays because what I saw over the years couldn't have occurred without implants attached to the jaw bone with titanium screws. Even Letterman asked him about this aspect. His teeth were large, perfectly formed and, like Billy himself, well maintained.

During the years we played together, it was common to see Billy rip the cover of a baseball off with his choppers. He would make a gouge with incisors and then grab the cover

197

with everything but his molars and dismantle the ball. This was always done to amuse and not out of anger. Anger he would take out on other things, mostly wooden items such as his bat that had failed him. One Sunday afternoon in Elmira produced a classic memory.

We had an unusually large crowd of three thousand in the stands and everyone wanted to put forth a little bit of extra effort. Fans do provide an incentive that is directly tied into a player's ego. All professional athletes have something wired in different than the average person or, more importantly, their competition who won't survive. The differences were subtle, but noticeable to me over time. Billy had one of those unbelievably bad days and snapped. Even though this was our fourth season together, I had never seen this happen before.

Scripture was an adequate third baseman but limited in range. His strength was anticipation on every pitch as to variables and where he should place himself. Like a super computer, every factor was being processed constantly. Who was the batter, what type of pitch had been called for, was the pitcher tiring, what were the circumstances of runners on base, what direction was the wind blowing, how close was the dugout to his right, who was the umpire observing the line, was the popcorn salesman in the first row going to present an interference problem if he had to lean over the railing, etc. This analysis occurred during each and every pitch.

The analytical ability carried over into other parts of his life. When Billy was summonsed for an Army physical he prepared in the same meticulous manner because if he were to be drafted it would be the end of his career. Since he was slightly hard of hearing due to the firing of various weapons over the years, he came up with a plan. His examining office was very small and the physical would be over quickly.

Scripture went to a friend's farm and fired off several boxes of shotgun shells between two barns that produced a concussive effect on his ear drums. He hopped into his car and within a short time underwent a physical and flunked the hearing test. Just borderline on the testing, but enough to put him in a category that could possibly get him drafted. Now comes the genius of the person.

Several months later, the draft board called him back for retesting. This was not uncommon for the time because all services were trying to come up with enough warm bodies to feed the war. No problem for Billy. He went between the same two barns, fired off the same amount of rounds, went in for the same examination, with the same results.

This particular black day in Elmira he committed three errors allowing many unearned runs and every at bat was humiliating. The final straw came when Billy struck out, taking a called third strike that was so hittable the catcher started coming out of his crouch anticipating a certain base hit. Instead, the ball settled into his mitt and the umpire gave a delayed, almost apologetic, call of "Strike three!" This stuff happens all the time to the best of hitters and they just shrug it off and mentally prepare for the next at bat.

Since this was the third out, the changeover started but Billy remained rooted in the batter box staring toward center field with the bat on his right shoulder. Our catcher approached home plate but Scripture stood his ground. Slowly he turned and came towards the dugout dragging the bat as if he were plowing a furrow with everyone watching this action. Because the main body of our club had returned to the field and he was the designated hitter, I was one of the few remaining when Billy fixed his stare on me.

What I saw was frightening because it was that of someone completely out of control with his emotions. After a few seconds, he erupted with a scream that can only be described as animal. He leaped from the top steps and fell to his knees in front of the bench. From there he proceeded to bite large chunks out of the pine. Most in the dugout moved toward the clubhouse, but I remained. I had to follow this to the end in order to understand what had happened to my friend.

After chewing on the bench for thirty seconds he stopped. I was seated no more than three feet away and the only player crazy enough to be near. Slowly Billy turned and looked up at me with an expression that can only best be described as that of Jack Nicholson in "The Shining" when he broke through the front door of the hotel and offered, "Here's Johnny!." "I'm really having a crappy day", was all Scripture had to offer.

Since Billy had stopped feeding on the wood, it seemed appropriate to have some type of normal conversation. I asked, "Did the ump blow the call?" This was the only thing I could come up with. "No, the pitch was the best I've seen in a long time and I couldn't pull the trigger. I had flashbacks to Wake when it would have been launched." All of a sudden we were having a lucid, rational, explanation as to what had just happened. Unfortunately, I was the only one who heard it. The manager's daily report to Baltimore couldn't have included this information.

Personal dress and appearance were very important to Scripture. Even though there was no dress code below the AAA level, he dressed as if he were in the major leagues always wearing a sport coat, perfectly pressed trousers and gleaming wing tipped shoes. This was someone on his way to the show.

We had a heavy overnight rainstorm in Elmira that possibly might cause a cancellation of the game, but with no actual rain out declared, we were obligated to show up and wait. Everyone was at the park except Billy and just minutes before the scheduled time, in he walked. The game had been called but he couldn't have known. His attire was perfect except for one thing. Scripture was covered with mud from his wing tips to his tie.

The house he was renting for the season was far out in the country and a personal vendetta had developed against a ground hog. When I saw the classic movie, "Caddy Shack", Bill Murray's character jumped out on the screen as Scripture. Billy was an avid hunter back in Virginia Beach and later went on, after his baseball career, to become one of America's top trap shooters. He had been trying to shoot this critter for weeks.

Before leaving for the park his opportunity surfaced and without regard for his clothing, Scripture began a slow, belly down crawl for more than thirty yards. Just as he drew a bead on his target, a stray dog charged the hole and down went his quarry. Billy lay silent for more than half an hour until it was apparent his goal couldn't be reached. The game came in second as to priority but, since we were rained out, no fine was levied. He dodged a bullet but added to his mystique.

Our only stint living together was 1966 in Stockton, California. We had played the previous year in Kennewick, Washington, but Billy was with his wife, Glenda. I can't remember why he was alone at this point and somehow, we ended up with a stray roommate by the name of Neale Blasé. a local radio announcer. Neale went on to achieve major league status in his profession by working at some of the top stations in the country.

For this summer, we were a perfect triangular odd couple. I cooked and Neale didn't mind washing dishes. Billy gladly got out of our way and enjoyed gourmet meals. Our professions matched up perfectly since Neale's night gig at the station allowed him use of the apartment after we left for the park at five. Occasionally we would find female undergarments left behind when we returned after the game. We just had a ball all summer long.

The three of us decided we couldn't handle normal housekeeping chores and wished to hire someone. Our landlady knew the perfect person who cleaned many of the units where we stayed. This merry maid arrived mid afternoon and we showed her where the cleaning supplies were. Because she was Hispanic and spoke little English, it took time to fully convey what we wanted. But with hand gestures and motions, the job requirements were established and we resumed our tanning by the pool.

Fifteen minutes later, a scream came from our apartment and because the door was open it reverberated throughout the complex. Our maid was running down the stairway toward the parking lot with her hands flaying above her head. None of us understood her language and had no clue as to what had happened. Our first thought was some animal had attacked her, but this couldn't be as the only thing we had seen were a couple of ants. It wasn't until the following day, through our landlady, did we find out what had happened.

Billy was not only a skilled hunter but also a master carver of wood. During the baseball season he would produce many beautiful heads of both ducks and geese. When we played together in Rochester, it was amazing to watch him whittle during flights and never harm himself. Heads would be mated with bodies in the off season. In our apartment the beasts had been stored in the linen closet and there were four shelves lined with sixty, perfectly aligned, eyeless heads facing forward.

As our lady busied herself she opened the closet out of curiosity. The shock was too much to handle and her immediate judgment was we were associates of the Devil. Off she went never to return, even though we brought our landlady into the picture to explain. After this encounter, we collectively decided the apartment would stay dirty during our stay.

I was the recipient of a win only achievable because of Scripture's incredible mental dexterity. The game was in the seventh inning and mine to lose since the score was tied. A runner was in scoring position and there were two men out. The batter hit a ball hard down the left field line that everyone knew had a chance of being a home run. Billy ran back and jumped. He crashed into the wooden fence coming down as if he were badly injured. Since this was a typical minor league stadium of the era and lighting was poor, it was uncertain as to what had happened. Umpiring crews at this level only had two assigned per game and a lot of territory to cover.

Billy had leaped as high as he could, slamming against the fence. If he had a ball in his glove when he came down, the batter was out. Slowly Scripture rose to his feet clutching his side. The umpire raced out to make the call and was shown the ball by our injured outfielder. Up went his arm signaling an out and all hell broke out. The opposing manager charged the poor umpire who made the call, totally out of position and without a clue. The closing argument in the case had been provided by the evidence. Scripture had leaped upward and once he stood up there was a ball in his glove. All pitchers know the outcome of a bad pitch. This ball had been hit out of the park and I knew this.

Scripture settled into the dugout accepting congratulations for his fine catch, but I knew differently. No one but me saw him go to the bag housing practice balls. Staring straight ahead, Billy slipped a ball into the center of his glove. The home plate umpire, now under duress from the opposing manager, came to the dugout demanding to see the ball in Billy's glove. There it was with scuffed marks just like a game ball should be. Final out, let's get on with the game but I had to find out, "How'd you do that?"

Billy told me he sometimes carried a practice ball in his right rear pocket just in case there was an opportunity where he could produce this magic trick. En route to the dugout he flipped this ball to a fan along the left field bleachers requiring just a slight shift in direction. It illustrates the division between the ordinary and baseball genius, which Scripture was. The next inning we scored a run and I was a winner courtesy of his sleight of hand.

The final day on a road trip to Salem, Oregon in 1965 almost proved to be fatal for Billy. We were rained out and our bus immediately headed for home arriving at three am instead of eight. There were a number of players staying at our complex, including Cal Ripken and his family. My apartment was on the second floor directly above Billy and Glenda. We all said goodnight quietly and settled in. Had I been married, I'm sure a phone call advising my wife of the change in arrival time would have been made. Apparently, it didn't cross Scripture's mind.

"Glenda, don't shoot!" This is what I heard as I was about to close my door. Even though you feel comfortable with personal relationships, there still exists the possibility of something sinister. I jumped the railing landing at the front door behind Billy. Glenda was in the darkness of a far corner of their living room holding a gun aimed directly in the line of sight for both of us. A few seconds allowed Glenda to move from dream state to reality and she came rushing forward with tears in her eyes hugging Billy, not seeing my retreat.

Scripture had purchased a pistol the week before our trip for her protection but hadn't had the time to give instructions except for how to load and shoot. I was unable to sleep that night as this was the one and only time to ever face a gun aimed with intent to harm.

Everyone in professional sports is assigned a nickname by either his teammates or the media. "Creeper" was that attached to Billy by Hank King after our playing back to back seasons together and the title accurately described the mysterious side of our teammate. Hank's attempts to track Scripture's nocturnal movements on road trips met with no success making us wonder if he might apply this obsession to the rest of the team.

The May 4, 1987 edition of Sports Illustrated contained a major piece written by John Garrity and deserves a republishing. Garrity is now a senior writer with Sports

Illustrated. Few players reach this level of importance in their sport without reaching the top, but to have one of the oldest and most respected publications dedicate a major amount of print to their memory is impressive.

It'll be midnight in the hotel bar when they start telling Billy Scripture stories. One baseball man will set down his margarita and say, "Remember when ol' Billy Scripture stormed out of the dugout with a gun and shot that seven foot rattlesnake on the mound in Sarasota?" "Yeah, and he turned up the next day wearing a snake skin belt and hat band!" Another will say, "Did you hear about the time in Columbus when Billy climbed the tower in right field and did chin ups from the light rack?"

The laughter will bring the waitress over to find out what's so funny, and a baseball man will say, "Sweetheart, we're talking about a fellow who was so tough he used to bite the covers off baseballs. He was so strong you could put six 200 pound ballplayers on a table and he'd lift the whole load on his back." "I've heard of him," she'll say, "Paul Bunyan, right?"

And that'll prompt them to tell the original Billy Scripture story: How when he was an All America outfielder at Wake Forest University, he heard that cutting wood was the best exercise for a hitter, so he went out into the woods and felled giant white oak trees by moonlight. CHUNK-CHUNK-CHUNK.

"You talk about hot water! By the time they caught him, Billy had cut down half the hardwoods in the campus preserve." "He couldn't pay for the damage, so as punishment they made him cut the trees into firewood for the faculty. He about got expelled!"

Billy Scripture, baseball manager, wood chopper, world class trap shooter, hunting guide, champion cusser. Spent nine years as a player in the Orioles and Mets organizations; became a minor league manager for the

Royals, got fired; joined the Pirates organization, didn't like the contract they offered and disappeared. "Think he's got a gun shop in Virginia Beach," says a writer covering the International League. "Last I heard, he was managing someplace in New Hampshire," says an ex-player, "but he may be out of baseball now."

And still the stories. How Scripture would straddle home plate and let a pitching machine bounce fastballs off his chest. How he would have several ballplayers hold one end of a fungo bat while he twisted the other end till the bat splintered.

A major league general manager says, "I once saw him bite a piece out of the bench, just to show how strong he was." A big league trainer says, "You know how they bundle up newspapers with heavy gauge wire? Billy would pick up a stack and bite the wire off."

Scripture, you might decide, is a myth. Indeed, THE BASEBALL ENCYCLOPEDIA, which lists all the players who ever played major league ball, has no entry for him. You won't find his name in an Orioles, a Mets, a Royals or a Pirates media guide. Directory assistance in Virginia Beach, Va. never heard of him. ("I show an EARL Scripture. Could that be your party?")

You have to dig. There is a tiny Scorecard item in the July 7, 1975, SPORTS ILLUSTRATED about the manager of a last place Southern League team who took out his frustration by chewing the covers off baseballs. ("Only lost one molar so far, and that's a whole lot less expensive than an ulcer operation.")

If you don't mind dust, there are old organization books in a back room at Royals Stadium in Kansas City. They show that an Earl Wayne Scripture Jr. ("nickname—Bill") was once the Royals minor league coordinator of instruction; that he was a 5' 9", 200 pound man of Scottish-English descent, born in Pensacola, Fla., who trained Labrador retrievers as a hobby; that he played a summer of semipro ball for the Alaska Goldpanners of Fairbanks; and that in 1967 he led the Eastern League in times hit by pitched balls.

And somewhere in the vaults of the National Broadcasting Company there is probably still a videotape of a flaky catcher showing baseball announcer Joe Garagiola how to bunt holding the bat VERTICALLY instead of horizontally. ("Hey, the ball can't hit your face. The bat's in the way.")

But those who knew him don't have to dig for memories of Scripture. "He's about on the edge of folklore," says Royals trainer Mickey Cobb. "The first time I saw him, I was visually stunned by the way he was built. He looked like he was etched out of stone. Massive jaw structure, flat stomach, thick hands....a shaved head. He was very fastidious. His uniform had a crease in it, and his helmet had to be just so.

"He was tough, maybe the toughest I've ever seen. I remember a time when he had 19 blisters on one hand from hitting. He just came in and poured alcohol on it. No Band-Aids. Other times, he would deliberately have someone hit flies out to the warning track so he could practice running full speed into the chain link fence. A crazy man? A sociopath? "Naw, Cobb says. "Personally, I found him to be a great joy."

"He wasn't a giant," recalls Pirates player development director Buzzy Keller, "but you talk about WOUND tight, I've seen him take a fungo bat and break it on his chest. A show off? A hot dog? Keller shakes his head. "He wasn't a kook by any stretch of the imagination. He was a very, very dedicated instructor."

"The most consistent thing about him," counters Royals general manager John Scheurholtz, "is that he got fired all the time. His priorities in life were; one, shooting skeet; two, dogs; and then baseball. He's not so remarkable—just

bizarre." Schuerholtz shrugs. "He WAS a good baseball man, I'll give him that."

Branch B. Rickey, minor league director for the Pirates, says of Scripture, "There were people who would complain that he was tough to work with, but there was never any question about his competence as an instructor or manager. Almost everybody remembers him fondly. It's just that Billy's singularness of purpose sometimes clashed with the aims of individual minor league franchises. With Bill, there was not a lot of accommodation to the owner's needs." Actually, the most consistent thing about Billy Scripture is this; Baseball people talk about him as if he were dead.

But, he's not. Here he is now, in fact, working in a closet sized room in the steel and cinder block shell house at the Orange County Trap and Skeet Club in Orlando, Fla. Black cowboy hat, blue jeans, boots, a polo shirt stretched over massive shoulders and a no longer flat stomach. A 20 diamond gold bracelet engraved with his nickname, "Billy"

It is four in the afternoon, and the 45 year old Scripture has been at it since before dawn, 12 hours straight, and he will continue till near midnight, keeping targets flying for prosperous snowbirds competing in a week long trapshooting tournament, Orlando's link in the Florida Chain Shoot. Neither the muffled blasts of nearby shotguns nor the news he is 400 boxes short of targets for the weekend shakes his calm. Unlike the old days, Scripture is not about to eat a baseball or climb a light tower.

"Hey, I'm sane and sober now," he says, striking a match to light a thin cigar. The tiny phosphorus flare illuminates the labels of cans on a shelf by his head: BALL POWDER...SMOKELESS POWDER...FLAMMABLE. He shakes out the match. "Someone's always runnin' in here sayin' there's a problem." He blows a cloud of smoke. "There's no problem. I haven't an idea where I'm gonna get 400 boxes of targets, but I'll get 'em, I'll get 'em if I have to effing invent 'em."

There's nothing in Scripture's manner to suggest he has been exiled, though you might expect it from a man who has been living in a hotel since May of '86, when he took over management of the gun club. "I didn't get tired of baseball," he says. "wasn't burned out. I just wanted to shoot full time." He nods toward the storeroom door, on which is written; THERE IS NO SECOND PLACE...EVER. "You have to have a hell of lot of determination to win in this game, just like baseball. You line up toe to toe and put your money on the line." Plus, there's something to be said for a life free from organizational inertia and red tape. "Sometimes I thought baseball was just an effing game of perpetual ignorance. You could come up with a better way to do something and they still wouldn't change their minds. 'Cause that's the way it had always been done. Baseball is full of people who manage scared, play scared and lose scared.'

He pushes his hat back on his head. "I probably couldn't manage in baseball today, because I'm probably the most hard nosed s.o.b. in the world. A lot of managers are basically excuse makers. That is an effing weakness. A character flaw. I love shooting, because this is a no-excuse environment. You either hit that sucker or you don't."

The door opens and Glenda Scripture, Earl's wife, steps in. She is down for the week from their home in Virginia Beach to serve as tournament cashier, taking entry fees and paying out cash prizes to the daily winners. Behind her is a red faced, beefy shooter with a complaint about a scorekeeper/puller. In the nearby clubhouse, card players laugh raucously.

Scripture calmly takes care of business and then heads for his red pickup truck. "You think the damned baseball players are crazy," he says with a grin, "you oughta see some of these people!" Another shooter, who has just come from the scoreboard, watches with admiration as Scripture hops into the truck. Scripture is the winner of that *afternoon's 50 pairs doubles, an event in which the shooter fires at pairs of targets released simultaneously in different directions. His score: 99 out of 100. "Earl put the hurt on 'em, didn't he? Ninety nine, that's damn good shooting."*

The next afternoon, Scripture competes in the day long singles championship—200 targets at 16 yards on eight different fields. The gun club's layout and ambiance are that of a golf driving range, except that these shooting sticks are made by Perazzi and Ljutic and cost $3,000 to $4,000 each. Expensive campers and RV's crowd the gravel lot behind the firing line. "There's no poor people in this game," Scripture explains, cruising in a golf cart behind the shooters. "You have to have a lot of money and freedom to pursue it. Otherwise, you're just a local club shooter."

Scripture is no local club shooter. His Amateur Trapshooting classification is the highest, AA-27-AA. The double A's mean he averages at least 97x100 in doubles; the 27 means he shoots from 27 yards, the longest distance, in handicap events. From 1981 to 1983, during a sabbatical from baseball, Scripture won four Virginia state championships—two singles and two all arounds. (He took the 1982 singles trophy with a perfect 200x200).

It's difficult to translate these scores into dollars. Unlike professional golfers, serious trap shooters put up their own money for tournament prizes in a complicated wagering system. There is no official earnings list, and it's like anybody's guess who is making how much. "I don't like to talk about the money," Scripture says. "You alarm some people and tick others off. I'll say this; The average shooter, if he takes a leave of absence from his job to try this full-time, he'll be back in 30 days. Very few people can truthfully say they make a living shooting. There's a handful of men making very good money, maybe 9 or 10." Is Scripture one of them? He pulls his down over his eyes. "I ain't sayin'."

He does not hesitate, however, when asked whether he was better at baseball or shooting. "MUCH better shooter.

Baseball was hard for me. I had some good college years that don't amount to a hill of beans. But, I had very limited ability. I was proud I got as much out of my ability as I did."
Shooting came easier to Scripture, who grew up on a South Carolina tobacco farm surrounded by woods and game. "My dad could shoot, and he taught me most of what I know."

Scripture parks the cart at Field 3 for the next round of 25 targets. The firing is brisk, each man yelling "Pull!"—or in Scripture's case, grunting "Yeuhhmph!"—firing and reloading. Shooters change stations five times per round; the various stations, combined with the 72 angles in the "fan" of the trap launcher, simulate the unpredictability of real birds rising from the brush. Spent shells surround the shooters' target fragments littering the field.

Scripture misses three targets in this round. "I'm not shooting anywhere near my potential now," he says, returning to the cart. "It's the same as golf. If a guy wants to be a good tournament shooter, that's got to be his first priority."

Guiding the cart to another field, Scripture pulls up behind four burly adults and a curly haired kin in jeans and T-shirt who is barely a hand taller than his shotgun. The boy is Scripture's 13 year old son, Jason, vacationing from Virginia Beach so he can embarrass his elders. "I really believe Jason's gonna be an outstanding shooter," his father says. "He's already won a couple of major handicaps. Shot their asses off." He watches approvingly as his son shatters 24 out of 25 targets. "Of course, he doesn't know what pressure is yet, 'cause I'm paying for everything. He's just farting around."

As shooters gather around him and exchange gun talk, it's plain his reputations as a teacher has followed him from baseball. "He can teach anything," says Cynthia Sutton, a young woman who has just come off the firing line. Scripture shrugs off the compliment. "Teaching is such a simple damn thing. I've never understood why people in baseball have so much trouble with that. You must slow it down, break down the mechanical motor skills, then you put it back together."

He learned that lesson first in the Orioles farm system, playing for managers like Cal Ripken, Joe Altobelli, Darrell Johnson and Billy Demars. The lesson was reinforced at the Royals short-lived but innovative Baseball Academy in Sarasota. Scripture studied and taught baseball fundamentals there alongside the late Charlie Lau.

"I loved the Academy environment. Charlie and I sat and talked for days, watched tapes, broke everything down. That's what made him such a great batting coach." Scripture stops the cart. "Baseball would do well to make sure they have the best people at the rookie league level. That first manager makes a hell of an impression on those kids."

It's Scripture's turn to shoot again, and this time he hits all 25 targets. After he returns to the cart, an obvious question arises: Which is the easier target, a baseball or a clay pigeon? "Well, I tell ya," he says, reaching for a cigar, "I can hit these, and I couldn't hit a curveball, so these must be easier." COULDN'T HIT A CURVEBALL?

Although he played five seasons in Triple A, Billy Scripture never had the proverbial cup of coffee in the majors. "It was an effing struggle to play," he concedes. "The ball always fell a foot short." His lifetime average was .252. His managerial record, measured in wins and losses, was similarly undistinguished. The sign on the door may say, "There is no second place...ever," but second place is the highest a Billy Scripture led team ever finished.

"He was always into self improvement techniques," says Rickey. "He jumped into psycho cybernetics and then into visualization, and I can't remember what else." Rickey recalls a restaurant dinner with Scripture years ago.

While they talked, Scripture's eyes remained fixed on a candle in the middle of the table. He would perform eye *exercises like that—following the tip of the flame, trying to hold his concentration while talking normally."*

Scripture trained and toughened his body, too, with weights and old fashioned calisthenics—thousands and thousands of push ups, sit ups and knee bends. Like Watergate conspirator G. Gordon Liddy, who tested himself by holding his palm to a flame till the flesh was scorched, Scripture abused his body, saying, *"if you're going to be a great athlete, you've got to withstand pain."* He established a high standard of personal courage, says the Royals' Cobb,

"I never saw him duck away from a pitch. He would simply move his head out of the way as the pitch went by his nose." Others remember his killing the rattlesnake, not with a gun on the mound, but with a fungo bat at the warning track, or even with his bare hands by the locker room.

Scripture encouraged players to follow his example. He would pay the player who broke up a double play at second. He would put catchers in full gear and hit line drives at them from 40 feet. *"He absolutely scared them to death at first,"* says Keller. *"It was his way of getting their attention."* Once he had their attention, it was a different story. *"He had incredible patience and compassion."* says Rickey. *"You just didn't see him blow up with players, just as he didn't with his own children."*

Rickey tells the story of Doug Frobel, a former Pirates outfielder who played for Scripture at Charleston, S.C., in 1978. Rickey had made a post game dinner appointment with the manager, and he remembers watching as Charleston lost a heart breaker in which Frobel failed at the plate and mishandled several balls in the outfield. Afterward, Rickey waited outside the locker room for 30 minutes before asking a departing player if Scripture was ready. *"No, he's out on the field,"* he was told.

Outside, the stadium lights were still on—a costly indulgence for a minor league club—and Scripture, in uniform, was kneeling in front of home plate, soft tossing baseballs to Frobel, who tried to drive them to the opposite field.

"I just sat and watched," Rickey says. "There were about a hundred balls in the bucket, and when they had exhausted it, they walked out and picked them all up, talking softly. Then they came back and started again. And over the next half hour, I watched them go through three buckets of baseballs.

"Now it gets to be a quarter till 12, the lights are still on. Bill picks up his fungo bat, sends Frobel into the outfield and starts hitting high fly balls, as only Bill can hit them. Frobel missed a lot of them, and Bill walked out to talk some more. When he brought the bucket back and started to hit another hundred, I finally yelled, "Bill, are we going to dinner?" Bill looked at me, and without a word he waved Frobel in and turned off the lights."

Ultimately, Frobel went on to accomplish what Scripture never did: He reached the majors. Rickey gives partial credit to the manager. "I never saw anybody with the kind of willingness to work with a struggling players. That he was missing dinner was of no concern to Bill; the cost of the lights was of no concern to him. Everybody talks about the crazy things, but what attracted me to Billy Scripture was the other stuff."

Willy Wilson, the Royals center fielder, played for Scripture at Jacksonville in 1976. "He had the most impact of all the coaches and managers I've had," Wilson says. "He was a wild man, but he never did anything to show off. He did it to teach you."

Wilson tells this story on himself. In August that year, Wilson was on the verge of quitting baseball. An injury had put him on crutches for two weeks, and now that he was back, Scripture wasn't playing him. After sitting out the first game of a doubleheader, Wilson had had enough. "I yanked *my uniform off and drove home, listening to the game on the radio."* Realizing that he had acted rashly, Wilson changed his mind and drove back to the ballpark, only to find that Scripture had put his uniform in the washing machine.

"He made me put my uniform on wet," Wilson recalls. "I sat on one end of the bench while he sat on the other end with this funny smile on his face. And then after the game he took me down the leftfield line for a talk."

During the talk Wilson learned why he wasn't playing: Scripture was keeping him healthy because the Royals were about to call him up for a September trial. "I still look up to Billy," Wilson says. "I never really had a father, but if I had a father, I'd want him to be like Billy Scripture."

Scripture hasn't forgotten that long ago conversation. He says he remembers everything about it—the exact spot where they stood, the wind, the lights, the temperature, everything. "I remember looking Willie right in the eye and saying, "Will, if you'll stay, you'll make a million dollars someday." He was in Double A, strugglin' his ass off, but I had a lot of faith in Willie as a person."

Scripture shakes his head. "I loved my players. That bull—you can't get close to the players? Hey, I ARGUED for 'em. I FOUGHT for 'em. Your successful manager always has a way of letting the players know, 'Hey, I'm for YOU. I'm here to help you.'"

This last is spoken back in the gun club shell house, late Saturday night. The shooters are asleep in hotel rooms or watching TV's in campers behind the clubhouse. Scripture sits on a case of shells and lights up another thin cigar. "I'll tell you what it would take to get me back in baseball, he says tossing the match out the door. "It would take a struggling organization that wanted to turn around its minor league system. I'd just like a hell of a good challenge. I'd like to take a can of worms and piece it together." The distant look in his eyes says that it will never happen.

"It's a horse bleep statement to say you're the last of a dying breed, but I played like there was no tomorrow. I ran into walls, fell into dugouts. It didn't matter when I played, where I played, how hot or how cold. I played baseball for the sheer effing love of playing. I always felt like if I had some ability, I would have been a hell of a ballplayer." Scripture gets to his feet. "That kind of talk—it's just running away from getting old."

Outside in the dark, he takes a deep breath and looks up at the stars. "I enjoy the hell out of what I'm doing now," he says. "I love it." He crosses the grass to a light tower and pulls a switch. Light floods a narrow patch of skeet field— the spokes and wheel of sidewalk, brown grass littered with target fragments, the squat shape of the trap house. The paint on the sidewalls is green, like ballpark paint. The light is ballpark light. Scripture looks around and nods contentedly. "It's just like walkin' into an empty ballpark, isn't it? Nothin' left but the pigeons and the popcorn."

NEW ORLEANS ROYALTY

My introduction to Lloyd (King) Fourroux came during my first day in spring training. I was standing in a chow line behind the biggest and meanest looking person in camp. I had been raised in the farmlands of Ohio unaware Cajuns had been placed on this earth by God.

Fourroux outweighed me by seventy pounds and as we moved forward in the line, I knew there was no hope for me in this business. There were many players with All American credentials but no one had the intimidating factor he presented. Sometime in the near future we would be facing each other and as luck would have it, my first chance to face the challenge came sooner than I wanted.

Lloyd's career started with the Orioles organization in 1960. In his second year he produced the kind of numbers Baltimore expected. Batting average of .298, 22 home runs, 94 RBI, and speed seldom seen in baseball. On the third day of camp we met.

King stepped in and I was facing my worst nightmare. Never had I seen a baseball bat held in the manner he did. It was cradled in the outermost bends of his fingers producing an action that was whip like. My catcher sensed fear since no matter what signal he put down, I remained motionless. I took a deep breath and accepted the signal for a curve ball. This pitch proved to be the bullet that shot down Lloyd's career in the Oriole's eyes. Once his weakness was revealed I finished him off with something dropping two feet straight down.

During my first camp I began to gather stories about Fourroux and continued over the years. Lloyd never bragged upon himself and specifically, not about being one of the best football players to come from Louisiana, possibly better than All American, Billy Cannon out of LSU. Somewhere his story gets murky as to why he didn't go to college. While many felt he was incapable of learning at this level, the truth was Fourroux had a high degree of hidden intelligence and a personality that few in the game possessed.

Several years ago I made contact with Lloyd prior to a vacation Mary and I had been looking forward to greatly. Fourroux had remarried and was with an absolute jewel by the name of Kathryn. She was educated, beautiful, and someone who had the capacity to make anyone feel there was a personal relationship cultivated over years, not days.

Our stay was at a four star hotel near Bourbon Street and Lloyd was about to provide one of the greatest insider tours of his city ever to be offered. The lobby was on the second floor and as we descended, Lloyd came into view from his shoes up and the image was incredible. His suit was white linen topped with a plantation owner's hat. I whispered to Mary, "Hang on to your butt, we're in for a ride."

We went directly to his house to meet Kathryn and have dinner, but I wasn't prepared for the experience. Their house was stylish and well decorated, courtesy of Lloyd's wife. This included an annex where he proudly showed me orchids being raised. I was stunned as to the change in this character and it was becoming hard to connect a link to our past.

Dinner was perfect and conversation had no connection to baseball. We learned Kathryn had a master's degree and was in charge of English programs in several parishes. Also, there was a slight mention, her father owned several paint franchises in the South. Given my fondness toward Lloyd, it seemed to be a perfect match in a relationship and I couldn't have been happier.

The most amazing aspect of our meal was, Lloyd had prepared everything himself. Even though we had known each other for years and he knew of my love for cooking, we never shared this interest. The shrimp recipe had secrecy fitting to the New Orleans scene and to this day, is one of the best I have ever tasted. Lloyd showed a broad grin when complimented and Kathryn handled the flow of conversation like a talk show hostess. I had to use their restroom and was directed down a hallway off the dining room.

I moved along twenty feet of photographs and framed miscellaneous items but what caught my eye was a small plaque declaring Lloyd had been inducted into the Louisiana Sports Hall of Fame. It put this person, who never reached any major status in either professional baseball or collegiate football, in the company of legendary people. Billy Cannon in football, Pete Maravich in basketball. I returned to our dinner table unable to ask questions until we were alone. The opportunity came when Lloyd showed me his orchids being grown in his small private greenhouse.

"Oh man, I forgot about all that stuff". There was no expansion on how this honor came about. Fourroux and I had the same respect for what we had been able to achieve, refusing to look back and lament as to what could have been.

Mary and I witnessed his New Orleans reputation first hand when we went club crawling. Our foursome started just off Bourbon Street in bars unknown to the average tourist. The neighborhoods were slightly questionable but when you had a guide as well known as Lloyd, all fear was removed.

Even though the time was early afternoon, jazz groups were playing unbelievable sets. Typically, players were old black musicians enjoying every minute doing what was their life's calling. Money wasn't important to them, just like our sport. It was entertainment and we all enjoyed applause after performing to the best of our abilities.

I was armed with many stories about the "King", but there was still doubt in my mind as to the large reputation he had carved within the state of Louisiana. Now I realize this was due to his lack of braggadocio. We had been surrounded by the upcoming new breed of players who had to advertise how great they were. I was "The Librarian" and Lloyd was the "King" and we were comfortable with who we really were.

Every stop we made, moving closer to Pat O'Brien's, the reaction to our entrance was always the same. When Lloyd was sighted, there was an immediate warm greeting by all. We were given preferred seating and complimentary drinks. Our host or hostess always took great pains to explain to those in the club who we were and why we were important.

When we reached O'Brien's it was early evening and our timing was perfect. We were able to have a table in the main room next to the dual piano players whose skills created entertainment energy. The requests might be for a college fight song or, because you're Irish, a "Danny Boy" sing along. We stayed far enough into the evening to accomplish my goal. Mary had the chance to visit this fabulous city but, more importantly, also experience the aura surrounding Lloyd. The plus for both of us was his wonderful new wife and it was obvious there was a deep love between the two.

The first chance I had to verify Lloyd's local reputation came on a transporter at Disney World. We were staying outside the resort and took a twenty minute shuttle ride with everyone stuffed together uncomfortably. The person next to me identified himself as having come from New Orleans. I asked, "By any chance, do you know someone by the name of Lloyd Fourroux?" The look on his face was amazing as his eyes showed a connection to my question, but he wasn't able to respond right away,

Finally he smiled and his words were someone of the region. "Sure I know Lloyd, ain't nobody in the state who don't know him." Quickly I explained my relationship and then began to probe. "Was he as great as they say in football?" My new friend answered in a beautiful Cajun patois.

"Let me tell you, I played middle linebacker in high school against him and the only thing I could do was pray he ran outside. When he did come up the middle he ran right over my ass and all I saw was the back of his jersey." Good enough for me since this tied into his reputation for speed. Every year in spring training Lloyd would be matched against the fastest in camp and large amounts of money were bet by coaches and scouts. Lloyd won more track meets than he lost.

We broke camp together heading for Stockton, California and it was difficult to understand dynamics affecting my life at this point. Not only had I survived Lloyd and the All American's but I was starting at the highest classification for a rookie. My first call after the assignment was to grandma because she would be the only person who could share my joy. She owned the first television in our neighborhood and we could watch our favorite Indian's player, Luke Easter.

1963 produced great statistics for Lloyd. His batting average was .285, 20 home runs and 104 RBI's. Another season with numbers Baltimore wanted. Since I had been shifted mid year to Appleton, I didn't see his late season performance that was a major factor in Stockton winning the pennant. I was excited about having played with someone I knew would surely land in the Hall of Fame.

We didn't join up again until the 1967 season in Elmira. By now Baltimore had given up on Lloyd as a hitter due to a high strikeout count each year. His conversion to pitching occurred the previous year in Miami, a bottom rung of classifications. His record was 17-10 with a 2.26 ERA. Outstanding numbers for someone who had converted to pitching mid career. The stats show he hit three home runs and I'll bet they were impressive as ever.

Now we were at the same level and two steps away from the major leagues. Since we were graybeards on the team, along with Howie Stethers, it was only natural the three of us would be roommates on the road. I was the youngest of the group at 24 but felt much older because of the struggle upward. Lloyd's stats were unbelievable this year doubling as a starter, reliever, pinch hitter and a record of 8-3 with a 1.77 ERA.

Lloyd's reputation with the ladies was almost too hard to believe. This got in the way with his first marriage, ultimately resulting in divorce. Never had I seen anyone smoother than Lloyd in this pursuit. The strange musical Cajun inflections, rough good looks, baseball stories, who could resist?

We were playing on the road in Reading, Pa. in the midst of a short losing streak. When the bus arrived at the hotel, our manager issued a statement. "There's a midnight curfew and anyone caught out will be fined $200." Since it was eleven this didn't allow for much more than catching something to eat, except for Lloyd.

Howie and I went a short distance from the motel and ate pizza returning to our room five minutes before curfew. I put my key in the lock and opened the door only to be stopped by the inside security chain. Since the room was in total darkness, we were uncertain whether Lloyd was alone. The curtains parted slightly and there was our roomie asking for more time before we would enter. What we didn't know, but suspected, there was a female in the room. She was a waitress getting off duty from a nearby tavern Lloyd had left no more than thirty minutes before. She bought into his smooth pitch and now we were facing a crisis.

As curfew approached we saw our manager starting his inspection far away from our room. Howie banged on the door but nothing happened. Malmberg was moving closer, but fortunately, Harry took the time to actually go into each room to conduct a body count. He was really pissed about the losing streak.

"What the hell are you guy's doing outside? Where's Fourroux?" I took the lead since Howie was about to swallow his cigarette. "He didn't feel good skipper. Came back right after the game and we didn't want to wake him up or smoke in the room." We were granted amnesty for a short period. "If I come back and you're not inside, you're out two hundred." This was enough incentive to start pounding on the door again.

Finally the security chain was released and the door opened. We entered our room only to find Lloyd alone. His new friend had panicked from the commotion, locking herself in the bathroom, with her clothes strewn about the room. It took thirty minutes for Fourroux to talk all of us out of a very difficult situation, but he did. I still wonder if we would have been hit with the fine had he required more time.

Elmira is a small community that has grown old over time. There is rich history, both good and bad, accompanied with uncertainty as to its future. Mark Twain wrote many of his famous books while living at Quarry Farm and is interred, along with his immediate family, in Woodlawn Cemetery.

On the downside, Elmira housed one of the largest and most lethal Civil War prison camps. The reputation came due to poor conditions and severe winters, producing a large number of deaths for captured southern soldiers. To this day, there is an annual pilgrimage by descendants from the Dixie states to honor their dead at Woodlawn.

When you are involved in a professional sport and arrive in Elmira, first impressions are mostly negative. My first sighting came after flying from spring training and wintering in California. My cab neared the center of the city and I asked, "Where's downtown"? We were in an area that appeared to be the oldest collection of structures ever seen in my travels. The driver turned and asked, "You're not from here are you?" "Not hardly" was my response. I checked into the Mark Twain Hotel and took a stroll.

After crossing the bridge dividing Elmira into north and south, I looked back and the view was shocking. The visible buildings were in such poor repair it would be only a short time before they would collapse in a domino effect. I went back to the hotel and called mom and dad. "I think I'm in the oldest city still standing in the United States!"

The taxi ride to the park the following day was emotional since now I was at a level only two steps removed from the major leagues. Given inner city deterioration, the stadium must be ready for condemnation and could be a negative influence over the course of the season. We turned onto a side street, traveling through a well maintained small home area on the south side of town. The cab made a right turn and I was staring at a structure that had no right to be there.

What I saw was a concrete stadium built during the 1930's with money from government programs designed to keep people employed during those difficult times. The land had been donated by a Mr. Dunn and hence, the ongoing name of Dunn Field. There is still a bronze statue of the gentlemen that has turned green over time but he watches over the parking lot with a benevolent look welcoming fans who could care less about history.

After being dropped off, I stood outside the gates allowing my mind to recycle. In front of me was the best showcase I was ever going to play in unless I made the major leagues. But the field surely couldn't compare to the outside. There had to be rocks in the infield dirt, grass infected with mites and a poor lighting system. I was right about the lights but this was corrected mid season.

Since I arrived early morning the only activity was that of vendors bringing supplies and all the entry gates were open. I climbed the ramp heading toward the center seating section and my reaction upon reaching the top is still hard to describe.

In front of me was a field so perfect it would have been the envy of any major league city. There wasn't a blade of dead grass and the infield dirt appeared to be as fine and smooth as Daytona's beaches. The outline of the base paths and coaching boxes were perfectly tailored unlike anything I had ever seen. The quality was due to the remaining efforts of the head grounds keeper, Pat Santarone. Baltimore was so impressed with his work he was hired as their chief in charge of turf the previous year. I ran down the ramp to find a pay phone to call my parents and reverse my thoughts about this season.

This is the scene Lloyd and I settled into. At various times we were heroes and had loyal followers both on and off the field. His main advantage over me was during the off season. I couldn't find a paying job since there were no marketable skills learned over the playing years. Lloyd was an electrician who could connect wires without killing himself or causing a structure to burn down. The local union loved him and Fourroux worked during the winter.

Our 1969 season produced a split organizational affiliation which was in vogue for a short period. We had players from the Orioles, San Diego and Kansas City on our roster. This made no sense since we trained at separate facilities, never played together at any level, and had no chemistry as a team.

We were surrounded by a generational gap almost a decade apart in actual ages. When questioned in casual conversation, few of our teammates knew any of the names or history of past baseball greats. There wasn't a person who knew Lefty Grove or Burleigh Grimes. Lloyd saw the need to exit mid season since he had endured enough abuse.

"Slim, can you help me with something?" We both had come to the park early and were alone. Fourroux was sitting on a chair in front of his locker with his head lowered and motionless. "Sure, what's up?" "Can you figure out what my career statistics are?" Immediately I knew his intent because this mismatched ignorant group had been planting irritating barbs all year. The most important link to the past was his prowess as a hitter and this year he didn't have a chance to even take batting practice.

Our front office had a library of Baseball Guides going back more than twenty years. This publication is important because each year has statistics for every professional level and is the definitive proof that one was even under contract.

I took my family on a visit to the Hall of Fame in Cooperstown, NY long after I had retired. I moved quickly through all the exhibits trying to find one connection placing me within this shrine. My last chance was in the room housing baseball reference books. All were enclosed under glass cases and it wasn't until viewing the last case did I find what I was looking for. A Baseball Guide from the 1964 season was open to the page detailing my outstanding year in Appleton with statistics for everyone to see.

Our family was in the room but had spread out amongst other visitors. My goal had been reached. I was officially in the Hall of Fame and no one could dispute it, at least for this day. Quietly, I gathered everyone and pointed to the evidence. To me this was just as important as having seen Babe Ruth's locker in the adjoining room.

It didn't take long to put Lloyd's numbers together and they shocked me. Fourroux's career, when he was strictly a hitter, was amazing. An average near .280 and 20 home runs per year. Combine this with his speed and overlooking defensive slights, there is no reason he shouldn't have his own collectible baseball card.

We were alone in the office and Lloyd was looking at my hand written numbers. He took a deep breath and said, "Slim, I'm out of here." Initially I didn't know if he meant the office, but looking into his eyes I knew what he meant. We sat motionless for an awkward period. I was witnessing a professional death for the first time. It wasn't until the following year I had to make my own decision about continuing. "Help me pack my bags." There was no reason for this request except for the friendship we shared. He didn't need my help but wanted someone to share the moment and memories.

I thought the process would be dragged out, but once Lloyd faced his locker it was as if he couldn't finish quickly enough. The grandest gesture was the placement of his jock strap on a hook near the door. I carried his bag to the parking lot acting as a valet. I was in awe of this character. He caused me to step back and evaluate myself. If Lloyd was gone, where did I stand?" My minor league credentials were even better than his.

Lloyd's afterlife started immediately in Elmira as he slipped into the community away from our small circle of fame. Occasionally, I would hear stories about his activities that seemed cockeyed, except for those familiar with the person. Olga was his first wife and a licensed hair stylist having a good base of clients. None of us knew much about her and there were never any social gatherings they attended together. She was truly a mystery woman to all of us.

The women of Lloyds' life were usually exotic and intelligent. What grated upon all our nerves was no woman was under the impression he was single. It didn't matter. There was this big Cajun in front of them with the smoothest line they had ever heard, and this is what they wanted.

One of the best Elmira bars of this era, and continues to be, is The Branch Office. Joe Mekos is the owner, possessing a broad sports intellect. This aspect, coupled with the protective net he provided for Lloyd, made for a perfect match. Somehow Joe kept in contact with either Lloyd or someone living in the New Orleans area providing the latest story about this person of interest.

When Fourroux was in Joe's tavern he was insulated from all his problems. If Olga was seen heading toward the bar, word spread quickly allowing Lloyd to slip away through the back door. This shows the love for this person in Elmira and also New Orleans. Olga left town after their divorce and Lloyd returned soon after to a support element in New Orleans he badly needed.

Several years later Lloyd was shot and the news traveled like a tsunami toward Elmira. Lloyd had been shot and survived. Rumors started both about the circumstances and his condition. It wasn't until he returned for a visit almost a year later would I learn the facts.

Something terrible happened in New Orleans but no one really knew. It wasn't possible to access information from newspapers, other than making a phone call, and nothing had filtered to the local paper about this story. Elmira's paper had a veteran sportswriter, Al Mallette, but even he was unaware as to the circumstances.

There was a watering hole on the way home that was comfortable to me for a brief stop. The bar was packed with a young crowd and after looking for a place to order a drink I saw a familiar face. Lloyd had returned to the area for some reason and was sitting by himself, talking to no one. My first reaction was to ignore him, but this was my friend who had a lot of answering to do in order to set the record straight in Elmira.

After moving to his right side I quietly offered, "King, what's going on?" and stepped back. Lloyd turned and as recognition set in, we returned to the last time we were together. "Slim, how y'all doin'?" I got to the point. "What happened when you got shot?"

"I went to a joint that was kind of rough and they didn't know me." He went on to describe a typical bar fight that broke out and Lloyd jumped in to break it up. Didn't know anyone, just wanted to solve a problem and get back to his drink. Management thanked him for his intervention and bought a complimentary drink before Lloyd left the bar to go home. Parked next to the curb was an older pickup and inside was one of the combatants.

"Hey asshole, get over here." When confronted with this type situation Lloyd never backed down from anyone. There were only a couple of times I witnessed this persona and it was frightening. Given his size and quickness, there were few who could compete and win. Had he taken up martial arts training there would have been a spot in Hollywood waiting.

Lloyd came to the right side of the truck. The driver pointed a .22 revolver firing several shots point blank and left the scene. All the bullets penetrated his body but only one was possibly life threatening, having nicked the wind pipe. The only logical thing in his mind was to drive to the nearest hospital. A typical emergency room scenario presented itself and even though he was wounded, Lloyd waited his turn in line with bullets lodged in his chest.

"Oh man, I've been shot!" This is what the admittance clerk heard from someone standing before her upright and without panic. Since the bullets were small caliber there was little visible to prove this declaration. Lloyd had the patience to explain what had happened and lifted his shirt to provide evidence. The clerk immediately called staff to take care of this person who had been considerate to others while waiting. It didn't matter Lloyd never reached the major leagues in baseball or any other sport; he will always be the "King of New Orleans".

WHITE LIGHTNING

My second spring training in Thomasville was nearing an end and I was enjoying the afternoon sun on a bench alone with my thoughts. A cab stopped in the driveway and two people got out. Two very ordinary people holding beer bottles in their hands.

Their trip across twenty yards of grass was like watching sailboats tacking into the wind. The smallest of the two and less likely to be a ball player offered an introduction. "Hi, I'm Dalko and this asshole is Frankie". I shook hands with the fastest pitcher ever to play professional baseball and gave a wave to Frank Bertaina as he weaved toward the front door.

Palmer and I were equal as to speed, but everyone talked about someone by the name of Dalkowski. Stories told in Thomasville about this person were hard to believe and couldn't be true, but they were, both on and off the field. Steve started camp this year training in Daytona Beach with Rochester and was sent down late for assignment to a lower league, along with Bertaina. The duo had taken more than twenty four hours to make a move requiring four. Baltimore ignored their behavior because of the collective talent in their left arms, and at this point it would have been difficult to apply any penalties for their actions.

How could the person standing before me generate speed that is still talked about today? Dalkowski was 5' 11" and weighed 170 pounds. Many in the game estimated his velocity to be as high as 110 mph and the best testimonial came from Cal Ripken, Sr. since he was Steve's catcher during the 1958 season in the Carolina League. Rip described his fastball as having so much upward movement, if it started chest high he had to turn and run to the screen because he couldn't move his mitt fast enough to catch up.

Doubters as to Steve's speed never faced a small, round object coming towards them in less than half a second from sixty feet. From my own experience, once 90 mph is reached two things happen. There is a high pitched sound produced by the raised seams on the ball cutting through air that is not there at a lower speed. And, if thrown from over the top, there is obvious lift much like that of a golf ball hit from the tee by a PGA professional achieving club head speed greater than the average amateur.

Dalkowski needed a helping hand to find his bed and I guided Steve to accommodations far different than what he was accustomed to at either the big league camp or Daytona. At four in the afternoon I tucked him in and rushed to tell all about Superman who looked more like a choir boy.

Ironically, since we had four separate practice fields, I never had a chance to see Steve throw during this camp. Palmer and I competed several times in addition to our staged contests on practice mounds. We were placed next to each other knowing our competitive instincts would result in perfectly timed release points and then the resultant pop in the catcher's mitt. There were no radar guns and this was how speed measurements were made. I refused to believe anything about Dalkowski's reputation since there was no reference point to compare.

To me, he was ancient history and Palmer and I were the stars of the future. Steve's feat of striking out 24, walking 18, hitting 4 batters and throwing 6 wild pitches in a 1957 game in Kingsport meant nothing. He also lost that contest by the score of 9-8. Steve AVERAGED almost 19 strikeouts per game but finished the year with a 1-8 record and an 8.13 ERA.

We left camp positioned properly. Steve was sent to Stockton and I went to Appleton. This legend had been demoted and offered further reinforcement to my own perceived value. Palmer was in Aberdeen, roughly the same talent level as Appleton and this is where I beat him in eight out of ten statistics, including strikeouts per game.

What Dalkowski achieved in Stockton during the 1964 season is interesting and I would have enjoyed being part of his season. Despite the history of wildness he become one of only two pitchers on this staff with a winning record of 8-4 but more importantly, an ERA of only 2.83. The inability to throw strikes had been conquered, but the question was how.

Steve became a shadow during the 1965 spring training camp with no apparent explanation after the excellent statistics in Stockton. His value to the Orioles had substantially diminished, becoming someone soon to depart the game. We competed on the mound this spring and he was below average putting him in a failure category for many reasons.

Once the roster was set for Tri-Cities, Steve became advisor since he had played there in 1961 for a team without a hint of talent. There wasn't a single player to reach the major leagues and the club record was 49-90. One pitcher, John Dewald, had an amazing year in reverse. Dewald was 4-21 with an ERA of 5.15 and Dalkowski followed with 3-12 and an ERA of 8.39. Steve was strangely quiet about this year except for one item. He insisted there would be a woman awaiting his arrival even though there had been a four year separation between the two.

Typically there is a one-week gap before games, allowing everyone to find apartments and settle within the community. Several of us, including Cal Ripken, found a complex outside Kennewick. Dalkowski found a hole somewhere and only those who gave him rides knew where he lived. But it didn't matter since he had become just ordinary. His greatest value was sharing important local knowledge, which included apartments, restaurants, and bars.

After several days of intense practice under Ripken we were ready to have some fun. The season opener was still two days away but our club had come together as a group due to Ripken's management skills. Someone suggested going to a club in nearby Richland because it had class and was perfect to further the bonding process. The someone suggesting was Dalkowski since this particular club had been his base camp during the 1961 season.

Every player attended and the party moved to a level that isn't experienced very often before a season starts. All wanted to swap stories about how we got to this point in our careers producing funny anecdotes. Steve was sitting across from me facing the main entrance. His head tilted to the right and a broad grin developed. When I turned to see where he was looking, I was amazed at the picture. A woman matching Steve's "awaiting woman" description was standing in the door scanning the room. She was wearing a black cocktail dress with a hair style producing a Liz Taylor image.

"Boys, I told you she would come!" With that, Steve stood up and walked toward this beautiful person. There was no kiss, no handshake, no hugs, just a classic joining of arms as they left the building. It didn't matter to either she was married and provided credibility as to the stories told about Dalkowski and his amorous skills.

We were a powerhouse. In addition to the excellent pitching staff there were hitters and sluggers on the team. Six regulars produced an average of 3.4 runs per game and all our pitching performed up to preseason expectations

Power was the prime element for Earl Weaver's master plan of managing and Rip had such a team. Earl believed one at bat producing a home run would have a multiplying effect if there were men on base. His skills as a manager were how to mold his team into this perfect storm. There had to be excellent lead off batters reaching base, players willing to sacrifice themselves to move the runner over and then the big blast producing a psychological blow to the opposition. Shut the other team down with the best relief staff possible and the game was won.

Weaver's managerial ascension through the organization was through intimidation and in Thomasville it was easy to observe his tactics. Since we were housed in barracks connected to a common corridor, it was a simple matter to crouch below the windows of the "Bird's Nest" able to hear the selection process. Only a few had the nerve since it might be the end of their career being discussed. Cuts typically started at 9 pm, meaning most decision makers had been at the local Elks Club before the nightly meeting. The Nest had unlimited beer and after managers and scouts settled in, chaos usually ensued.

"Who the hell wants this guy and why"? Your career was controlled by alcohol and someone willing to stand up to that night's bully. Earl was the master manipulator molding teams he wanted since most managers yielded during the process. Weaver could also out drink everyone at these meetings. No one was able to eavesdrop on a nightly basis because of the possibility their name might be next. It was Baltimore's version of Russian Roullete and we waited for the early morning cut list to be posted next to the cafeteria door. At least you would get a final feeding before packing the suitcase.

Dalkowski immediately became a favorite of the fans but it was hard to understand the love since his record was miserable for the 1961 season. Helping to pull everything together was Cal Ripken. Rip was the perfect fit as far as giving Steve and the Orioles one last chance together. There were only three years separation in age and Cal had been his catcher when Steve's speed produced stories hard to imagine.

Our club in Kennewick was so poor there was no team bus and transportation for trips around the league was donated cars, the newest being ten years old If a vehicle broke down, the starting pitcher from that night's game stayed to oversee repairs, hoping to be reimbursed by the front office. This happened to me once in Portland, Oregon and it was two weeks before I saw my out of pocket money return. Fortunately, my landlord was a baseball fan and understanding when I couldn't come up with rent money on the first of the month.

Ripken encouraged a natural selection process to determine who would be in each car. It allowed friendships to form in small clusters as we rode around the northwest. This was important because we were to be together for long amounts of time on the road, unable to move away from personal conflicts. Each ride would have players dealing with their own successes or failures. Our travel wagon was driven by Herm Rathmann who didn't mind the long stretches at the wheel and also didn't drink.

One night on the return from Wenatchee to Kennewick, our car radio locked onto the Monitor Sports Network. "Hi everybody, this is Joe Garagiola and tonight's fifteen minutes is all about the legendary Steve Dalkowski. We'll be right back after this commercial message."

Our first trip to this city had been carefully analyzed by our crew. There was a need to find a tavern having enough frontal parking to allow stopping quickly without anyone noticing and we found one. I think, because of our car's veteran status, Rip allowed us to be last in the caravan and somewhat invisible. Two of us jumped from the car and ran into the bar looking for the owner or anyone who could handle our long term request for cold beer on short notice. The bartender turned out to be the owner who worked evenings and found our request to be amusing. We left a large poster with scheduled return dates circled in red. No other tavern could boast what would be happening and we noticed his patronage had increased every time we arrived.

As the season progressed, time away from the highway decreased significantly since we now put three people out of the car. One to locate the beer, one to throw money on the bar, one to impress patrons and extend an invitation for that night's game. We were in full uniform and over the course of the season we converted many to rooting for the Atoms instead of the local team.

Dalko was between Howie Stethers and me in the back seat well into a case of beer we were hauling in our antique Chevy wagon. The empty bottles were launched out the open rear window by Steve without concern for anyone following.

Garagiola returned to the broadcast. "Our feature tonight is all about Steve Dalkowski. I don't expect many to know who this person is but you should understand his importance to professional baseball." Joe went on to describe many of the legendary happenings attributed to Steve. Most were true and Steve would nod his head in the affirmative between swigs of beer. When something wasn't true, he became agitated and set the record straight right there in the car.

"I didn't rip the guy's ear off, just hit him on the earlobe and there was a lot of blood." In doing research, I found a description where the ear was torn off and had to be stitched back on. This came using a MSNBC website that posted an article written by some Connecticut sports writer.

He did win a bet in Stockton that he could throw a ball through the outfield fence with no warm up. When I played in Stockton my first year, the evidence was still there in the form of a patch job on the wall. During Joe's show, Steve provided all the information needed to reverse many of the untruths. The biggest story was given to me by Steve the following year after he was out of baseball and living in Stockton.

Salem, Oregon can be damp and cold in early spring. Unless you were selected to play for a team in the southern half of the country, there was no way to avoid the misery of not being able to feel your fingers during a game. I threw a shutout against the Pirates club in our road opener in 1967 giving up just three hits.

Since the temperature was nineteen degrees at the end of the game, I know all the batters from the third inning on didn't want to swing the bat. I had a gas hand warmer in my right rear pocket and reached for it after every pitch in order to feel the ball. The downside was I ended up with a burn blister on my right butt cheek, but it was worth it.

I jammed one batter in the eighth inning and he stood at home plate jumping up and down trying to escape the pain. It was embarrassing for both of us when I picked up the dribble and applied the tag while he was still in the batter's box. But, as they say in all professional sports, the playing field is level for all. Bullshit, it just plain hurts and isn't fun.

This night in Salem, we had a hard throwing right hander who could dominate a game if he was on. Steve was the exact opposite at this point in his career. Dalkowski was our next pitcher in rotation and required to keep a detailed log of every pitch and result during the course of the game. The theory was it would provide knowledge on how to pitch each batter the next night and was a discipline imposed by every major league organization.

I walked into the clubhouse to get warm and found Steve charting the game via radio. The bullpen was close to the dugout and it was reasonable Cal would assume the assignment was being done even though Dalkowski wasn't visible to him. "Slim, don't tell Rip I'm in here. I was freezing my ass off on the bench and this is stupid." Since I agreed with his logic, there was no conflict on my part.

We sat together for a couple of innings enjoying the warmth alone. When the announcer didn't provide the typical description such as, "Ball one, fastball low and away", Steve would bang the top of the radio and declare, "Shit, what was it?" Then he would settle down and record, in the proper slot, exactly what he would have thrown in the situation. It didn't matter all his pitches would be coming at the batter from a completely opposite angle since he was left handed. Without a trace of a smile, he handed the chart over to Rip after the game.

At this point in his life, Steve was rapidly descending both professionally and personally. Some small credit should be given for his abstinence from alcohol most nights prior to a start, but days in between were often embarrassing. This produced conflict among pitchers, since he was taking up a valuable slot in the starting rotation and also the organization. His many times repeated stories of the past had grown old with everyone, even Ripken.

This is a cutthroat business with a short life cycle and the only thing saving Steve was his personality and honesty. The honesty was shown every two weeks on pay day. After cashing his check he would approach each player asking how much money had been borrowed. Whatever amount was named he paid without question. This routine had been going on for the last three years of his career and everyone understood.

One of the most damaging stories is about Steve's IQ score of 65. This test is attributed to Weaver ordering every player on his 1963 Elmira team to submit to this abusive order. This was my first year in professional baseball and never was there a mention by any player as to this happening during my eight year career and is just a myth perpetuated over time.

Dalkowski developed a deep seated hatred toward all efforts to corral his talent both on and off the field. Weaver became an irritant to Steve because of these efforts and Earl's own personal weaknesses. To Steve, Weaver was forever "that little friggin midget." Steve never mentioned anything about this testing, and if it had occurred, he either would have been too hung over to understand questions or deliberately answered incorrectly to get back at Weaver.

References can be found about his speed being measured at the Aberdeen military facility in Maryland. Some stories describe this as an event arranged by the Orioles and those mentioning velocity vary in miles per hour. Consistent to the reporting is the mention Dalkowski threw without the benefit of a mound or baseball spikes.

Steve tells the story of being awakened early morning in his York, Pa. room by Weaver with an order to come to the lobby immediately. Since Dalkowski had been drinking all night it was both difficult to understand or resist the directive given by Earl.

Weaver had met a retired general at the York American Legion. Late in the evening an order was issued by this person to construct a device allowing newly developed laser beams to measure speed. The zone was extremely small and made of pine. Dalkowski said he couldn't throw one pitch through the measuring space after thirty minutes, badly splintering the wood. This scenario makes more sense than all other stories since it explains why Dalkowski would be throwing in street shoes.

Given his value, it is unlikely the front office would have arranged such a test and Steve would have proudly declared a measured mph in an era where no one knew how hard they threw, but wanted to know. This is why Baltimore placed Palmer and me on mounds together with velocity measured by sounds between release point and arrival time to the catcher's mitt. Considerable effort has been made to find film of Steve throwing but none has been found.

Ten years ago I was contacted by a major film documentary company requesting information about Dalkowski. I was someone who knew first person stories, along with others. Their focus was to highlight the effects of alcohol on professional athletes and Dalkowski was going to be their poster child. Nothing came of this because they missed the bigger picture about the person.

Dalkowski's problems created many opinions and few, except those who knew him intimately, could understand how simple he viewed life. Pro baseball provided him with everything needed since he was a teen growing up in New Britain, Ct. stealing bottles of vodka hiding them in a local park. His goals from this point in life were to get drunk, bed a woman and throw a baseball as hard as he could. When the end of his professional career with Baltimore came it was tragic and I was there for the final hours.

Late in the season I beat some club experiencing the typical high from winning. Unfortunately, there couldn't be much celebrating since we had an early morning departure for a road trip to Lewiston, Idaho. My plan was to stop on the way home at a tavern partially owned by Billy Harris. Harris had been hired by the Orioles to be a home only pitching coach and, outside of George Bamberger, had the keenest intellect as to the psychology of pitching I ever encountered.

Billy's professional career was strong and I tried over the course of our season to learn more. He only disclosed his proudest moment came in a start with the Brooklyn Dodgers in 1957 and Sandy Koufax came into relieve. Harris' instructions from Baltimore were to teach and that he did most effectively even though it was on a limited basis. He also is one of the nicest persons I met during my career.

The Playboy Tavern had the best pizza in Kennewick and a couple of drafts would be just right for a low key celebration prior to our early departure for Lewiston. Our apartment complex was only five minutes away and I knew my roommate would be asleep since he was fanatical about getting a good night's rest before a road trip.

There was one person I didn't want to see when I came through the front door. Dalkowski was there waiting for a friendly face to show up and I entered with no way to duck and run. Someone had provided transportation from the ball park to the tavern and dumped him.

Billy was behind the bar and after our initial greeting, it was apparent he didn't want to be any part of the rest of Steve's evening. This meant I would be Dalkowski's taxi from this point on and transportation was critical for Steve since he didn't have a driver's license. Stories about Steve's drinking and Baltimore's looking the other way surfaced one night in 1962.

Dalkowski was driving a new convertible on the outskirts of Elmira when police pulled him over for speeding. The owner of the car was a teammate asleep in the back seat trusting Steve to get him home safely. The officer made a decision to cut Steve a break since he was a Pioneer fan and intended to send him on his way without a ticket.

Unfortunately, Dalkowski put the gearshift into reverse and ran into the police car's front end resulting in suspension of his driving privileges in New York State. Steve offered this story to me as to why he never tried to regain a driver's license. In his mind, there was certainty he wouldn't survive if allowed to drive a motor vehicle.

Wives on our club refused to believe stories told by their husbands about Dalkowski. A challenge came from Sandy Fisher this season when she forced her husband and me to invite Steve for dinner after a Sunday afternoon home game. To our surprise, Steve was conversationally elegant and drank minimally. After Tom returned from giving him a ride home Sandy lit into us.

"You guys should be ashamed of yourselves! No way can the stories you tell be true. You all are jealous of him and want to tear him down. This is what I hate about baseball!" Maybe if we had taken Sandy bar hopping later in the evening she would have seen the Dr. Jekyll we all knew.

Steve spotted me before I could turn and leave unnoticed. "Slim, get your ass over here and let me buy you a beer". Since this was my game plan to begin with, I settled into the seat next to him. Harris was happy as responsibility for Steve was now mine and he could lock the doors and go home at closing. I was doomed, but only for the next twenty four hours. Steve's career with the Baltimore Orioles was over but neither of us knew this fact at the moment.

"Can you give me a ride downtown? There's a new dancer at a club and I promise, I'll find a ride home". Dalkowski's request had to be measured carefully. I was on a high from winning but also interested in seeing the latest go-go girl. If Steve kept his promise about the ride I could leave early and get some sleep.

Washington state law at this time prohibited moving about a tavern with drink in hand and required a server to transport. He or she picked up the drink and you followed pointing out the destination. If you wanted to move again, this process had to be repeated. Today it is hard to understand legislative logic of the time and we broke the law frequently this night.

Upon entering the tavern, Steve saw people vacating a position directly in front of the elevated stage where the dancers performed. "Buy us a beer, I'll grab the table". I obeyed the law and followed the waitress with beers to our prime position.

Almost immediately, the fresh talent was gyrating directly in front of our table. Very attractive, mini skirt, cleavage, and we had an upward view. My focus was so intense, I lost track of Steve due to the size of the club and it took awhile to find him in the darkness. I saw him waving me over to a large group that appeared to have more girls than guys. Steve's radar had locked onto a party and needed me for another ride.

The size of the party caught me off guard since I couldn't understand who would turn over three thousand square feet of his home to more than one hundred people, but this wasn't my problem. All feeling for time was lost since drinks were abundant and nobody had to transport them from point A to B. We could move about freely and cast out our best lines in hopes for a date this evening.

It was apparent Steve was on a roll since there were several attractive women listening to his every word. I was bottom trolling without success when a decision had to be made at three am. "Steve, I've got to get some sleep, we're leaving in a couple of hours."

"You son of a bitch, you're going to leave me here with no way to get home?" Key word in this question was "home" since I didn't have a clue as to where Steve lived. My route was five minutes away with no traffic and I wasn't going to wander around unfamiliar territory playing taxi. "Find a way because I'm out of here!" My feeling was Dalkowski would use his natural charm to find transportation and get lucky along the way as he usually did.

Four hours sleep proved to be far less than required and my traveling crew was trying to protect me because I hadn't shown up at the park to make the trip. Since there were so many vehicles involved instead of a team bus this was easy to do. When Rip declared it was time to leave, everyone got in their respective cars and left the parking lot in the agreed upon order without any head count.

Steve had arrived five minutes prior to departure and his driver was one of those I had seen just a few hours before at the party. The top on her convertible was down and after a long parting kiss, Dalkowski was ready for the trip. This was especially impressive since Rip was standing ten feet away. Given their long association, Cal just accepted the circumstances. Steve was there and it was time to get on the road.

I was so low key and predictable my absence wasn't noticed and the caravan left for Lewiston. Our car was missing an important member of the crew but there were plans to pick me up without anyone noticing. Rathman reduced speed gradually so the move away from the main road wasn't visible to Rip in the lead car.

Three people charged into the apartment since my roommate had left the door unlocked anticipating there would be a rescue attempt. I was sprawled on top of the bed covers still dressed in the same clothes from the previous night. Someone assembled my wardrobe for the next three days but his choices resulted in plaid shirts with striped pants. I would have blended well with the dress of San Francisco, but not Lewiston, Idaho. Pit stop time was less than three minutes and we were back on the road.

The first person coming into my apartment during the drill was Dalkowski. Apparently, I had been forgiven for leaving him and he wanted to make sure I was alright. Our refrigerator was next to the front entrance and Steve found a six pack of beer before leaving. He removed each can from the plastic ring, finding hiding places in his trench coat and trousers.

This was a beautiful day to travel and my plan was to catch up on lost sleep but wouldn't happen since Steve had to tell all about his night. His descriptive skills were strong in a strange, crude way. If Steve had ever reached major league level, sports writers around America would have encountered someone most unique. Dalkowski would have been incapable of deviating from what he truly believed at interview time or in the clubhouse with his fellow players.

Herm entered a construction project and the flag person assigned to slow traffic caught Dalkowski's attention as we entered his zone. It took some effort but Steve moved over baseball gear stowed in the rear and after dropping his pants, mooned this traffic coordinator.

The flag person abandoned his responsibilities and was sprinting toward our car, only slowing when he saw a large black man behind the wheel and the vehicle coming to a stop. This reaction emboldened Steve since he knew teammates were there for him and he had three more beers to drink. "My ass is better looking than your face!" The pursuer turned in defeat and went back to pick up his flag.

Our gypsy caravan arrived in Lewiston mid afternoon with a three hour respite before leaving for the park. This was typical timing for any road trip providing options, with most choosing either a nap or going to a movie. Steve took a different route on this trip since it took little persuasion for the hotel barber to close shop early. He was a fan from 1961, an alcoholic, and they joined together in the bar for the hours before we were to leave for the park.

Cars departed the hotel promptly at five with Steve on board but very quiet. I had found him in the bar just before we were to leave. He was just another player with problems and everyone was moving away from any personal relationship. Dalkowski was near death in professional baseball and it could be smelled, much like he did on the way to the park.

Batting practice for both teams typically was an hour allowing everyone to adequately warm up. Starting pitchers are afforded much needed exercise of their arms between starts and position players see live pitching minutes before the game. Since I knew Steve was potentially in trouble this night, I made a move toward our club house without anyone seeing my departure from the playing field.

I found Dalkowski in the shower naked, leaning against the wall with water washing vomit away. "Slim, help me. Rip can't see me like this!" With some difficulty, I moved Steve out of the shower placing him in a storage room that was never used. He had less than an hour to repair and since he was our starting pitcher the game's outcome was in question.

Steve appeared in the bullpen minutes before game time. Because this area was far removed from the dugout his only contact became his catcher. He had dressed in the storage room going directly to the right field corner with no indication there might be a problem. We were the visiting team and Lewiston took the field first leaving Dalkowski alone on the end of our bench.

Combining heat and humidity, Steve produced odors within the close confines of the dugout that were undeniable. A twenty foot separation from anyone developed, leaving this poor soul alone to face the night. Even Rip moved to the far left upper step to get away from not only the smell, but visual evidence of white foam on Dalskowski's thick hairs at throat level.

From the start, Steve was in command of every pitch and throwing harder than any of us had ever seen, except for Cal. Between innings his catcher quietly, and respectfully, complained about pain in catching Steve's fastball. The curve ball was downward and biting resulting in a complete game with double digit strikeouts and few walks. One of the strikeouts almost created a brawl.

Rick Monday had signed with the A's organization for a bonus in excess of $100,000 of Charley Finley's money and we all knew this. His first year statistics with Lewiston were, .271 and 13 home runs and he went on to play 19 years in the majors. I had no particular problem this season facing him and remember his striking out twice in my final game playoff victory.

"Hundred thousand dollars, my ass!" Dalkowski offered this taunt after throwing a rising fastball completely overpowering Monday to end an inning. It was obvious everything was clicking this night and old memories were being dredged up as to how good he once was.

Monday started to charge the mound but after finding half hearted response for a fight from his team he retreated. Steve's reputation was known by all and there was no need to empty the dugouts. The inning was over and so was Dalkowski's career with the Orioles.

It was time to celebrate our win and on the return to the hotel Steve asked if I would be his partner for the night. This was not an unusual request since there was no one else for him to turn to except me and I had just lent him twenty dollars. His performance raised questions in my mind and there was no hesitation in agreeing to join him.

Lewiston had the appearance and feel of being one of the last Wild West cities left in America since urban renewal and freeways were decades away and we were staying at the Lewis and Clark Hotel. Both the city and hotel were aging but provided a strong feeling as to their past. It took little imagination to see the legendary explorers traveling through and what they might have observed.

Ripken wisely placed every bar off limits within the city. Cowboys seldom mixed well with Native Americans, tourists or ball players. In order to party, one had to rent a cab and travel far from the comfort zone of our hotel. This was the only city I played in with the possibility of total team celibacy. We were staying at a hotel near a night club seating two hundred and a live band. Steve decided this is where we were going to celebrate his win and there was no negotiating

Females were in abundance and we had no worry about time except for our departure to the park the next day. Perfect seating became available at the center of the bar close to the dance floor. It was only eleven and we had three hours to find companionship for the evening and Steve was my leader.

Within fifteen minutes Dalkowski spun a web capturing two attractive females and the rest of our evening appeared to have promise. Typically, I wanted to explore my new friend's mind while Steve only wanted to know when his companion would return to his hotel room.

The live band allowed Dalkowski to showcase another talent few had an opportunity to see since he was usually too drunk to perform. Steve had dancing skills where, if matched with a proper partner, the floor would clear to allow center stage alone and this was one of those nights. Unfortunately with Steve there was always a cross over point when alcohol caused chaos. I heard a scream and a slap in that order. Steve had chosen this moment to whisper what his intentions were and fondle at the same time. He had slipped into an alcoholic stupor placing him in his hotel room and not the forbidden bar.

Within seconds we were surrounded by a group of large, square jawed, cowboys wearing great looking white Stetsons. Even though I was the only one in the bar wearing black horn-rimmed glasses, my aggressive drive kicked in. This is what allowed me to survive in professional baseball, the ability to command no matter what odds were in front of me.

My goal was to convince the bar everything was now under my control. Steve took direction after slipping into a mellow state after the slap. Grabbing the back of his shirt and belt, I marched towards the front door using him as a shield. The gauntlet we ran was similar to that in Louisville when Jerry Herron and I discovered we had entered a packed gay bar and he shouted, "These are a bunch of queers"! My only mistake was allowing Dalkowski to open the front door on our way out. There was a small circular window with one way glass and since we were heading away from our troubles I dropped my grip.

Steve decided, for whatever reason, our leaving required putting his fist through the door's window. Fortunately the intense crowd inside was gone allowing me to sprint one block to the hotel looking for help. This was a command decision on my part whether to leave a comrade or stay.

At this time of night I expected to see players hanging around the lobby but nobody was available to help. I reversed direction returning with less than five minutes having elapsed. A crime scene had developed in this short period and police cars were in front of the bar along with a large crowd. Somewhere in the middle was Steve alone. Lewiston police camped out in the same area each night because trouble usually started here.

Dalkowski found a homeless person urinating on the side of the building housing the bar while I returned to the hotel. Steve was incapable of coming up with a better defense other than accusing this person of breaking the window. Broken glass was on the sidewalk, not the bar interior, and police had their man. Instant payment for the window was demanded by the owners with an understanding they wouldn't press charges. I had twenty dollars in my jeans, enough to provide momentary bail.

Steve was able to walk without support on the return to the hotel and because he was silent I relaxed my guard, once again. We entered the elevator together and my night was to be over once I punched the button for our floor. Without saying a word, Dalkowski hit the button for the floor beneath our rooms and the doors opened.

"Come out, I know you're in there and want me!" He was able to deliver this message to five or six rooms, pounding on each door for emphasis. Steve had noted the floor assignment of an attractive woman when we checked in and now was in pursuit. Once I was able to put my arms around him he gave up allowing us to reenter the elevator unseen.

I slept in and it was early afternoon when the same elevator from the night before delivered me to the lobby. Ripken was seated on a sofa with a look of defeat on his face. This was shocking since Rip was the most upbeat and positive person I ever met in baseball. Our eyes made contact and he motioned for me to join him. "Slim, I had to release Dalkowski and you should know why". Ripken was a master at knowing team chemistry, just like Weaver. He knew, without questioning me once, I was one of few having a chance to possibly help with the reclamation project. But time had run out for Steve.

"The police came to the hotel this morning and told me what happened last night". He proceeded to give me their report and asked, "Is this the way it came down"? The facts were accurate and I offered confirmation. "I've been under strict orders from Baltimore to report anything major and they've finally given up on him."

It didn't take long for this information to sink in while we sat together in silence. Rip's head was lowered and I looked away while we gathered our thoughts. Rip was a person who could give an accurate measurement as to Steve's past potential and I was Dalkowski's only friend in life at this moment.

Dalkowski didn't have to suffer any embarrassment in front of the team since Rip had purchased a bus ticket for his return to Kennewick. He also arranged for someone to open the clubhouse and gather Steve's personal belongings. Wide spread assumption on our part was there would be no repayment of loans made since the greatest arm in the history of baseball was now gone and we wouldn't return home for another two days.

"Line up you sons of bitches, here I am"! Steve was in our locker room the first day home with a fist full of money. He moved from player to player with the same question, "How much did you give me?" Never had it entered his mind to take advantage of the situation. He wanted to square things with his teammates and move on. We began to compare notes after Steve left, finding everyone had reacted in the same way declaring ten cents on the dollar. Dalkowski was gone from our lives but we would retain memories few others would have, including Joe Garagiola. Dalkowski joined San Jose of the California League for the last portion of the season since there was a former connection with their manager. Unfortunately Steve's arm was gone and his career in professional baseball was officially over.

When a significant death occurs, journalism protocol requires the story to be framed with a black box containing a short synopsis of the person's life. Longer, detailed stories come later fully describing why such an honor was accorded.

The Sporting News is a national publication covering all major sports. Everyone hungered for their name to be mentioned in some way each week. My biggest disappointment came when I struck out four batters in one inning only to read the same had been done by a pitcher who had been demoted to Stockton the week before. Joe Rowden got the ink instead of me.

Knowing the importance of black lines surrounding an article, my eyes were drawn to the upper left portion of the Sporting News front page. A six inch, one column obituary announced the end of Steve's career. There was a single sentence about his release from professional baseball and then career statistics. This legend was gone but I didn't know Dalkowski would offer a secret from his past when we came together again the following year.

Banishment to Stockton in 1966 did provide a foundation for advancement as predicted by Bamberger in Fernandina Beach. I dominated the California League in most categories as I should have except for the worst statistic, losses. This almost allowed me to forget the 13 games lost by one run on the way to an 11-17 season for a team that finished more than thirty games out of first place.

I was the only returning member from Stockton's 1963 championship season and the paper identified me as a possible hope for this season. When confronted by reporters as to why I had returned after going 26-9 over the two previous seasons, there was no answer that would make sense. I was a slave to the system without an explanation as to how my career had been altered after a five-minute encounter with a drunken manager in Fernandina Beach.

One night our bat boy came to me before the game to say there was someone in the parking lot wanting to say hello. There stood Dalkowski with his characteristic, loopy grin and a face that resulted in nicknames of Moon Mullin, or Moon Man. I was in uniform and seeing this person shocked me into realizing how much a role reversal had taken place over the past year. I was still headed toward the major leagues and Steve was begging for something.

"Slim, can you meet me after the game? I'm working and doing good. Let's go out and have some fun". We shook hands with a guarantee I would be there. Since a typical game would put me at the bar around eleven, I expected Steve to be in a drunken condition allowing my early exit without worrying about transporting. His normal drinking pattern was to have three or four quick double martinis and settle into how much beer he could consume before a problem occurred.

"I have to tell you something I've never told anyone". This came after Dalkowski had been served his first drink for the evening and it was obvious he was focused on telling the story to someone he knew and trusted. I had been planning on something far less than being confessor to one of Steve's greatest sins in baseball.

"I never could have made the bigs, they'd have their hooks in me". I didn't recognize what this meant and remained silent. It was obvious more was to come but there could be no interruption on my part. The longer we sat silent it became apparent the story was larger than I could have imagined.

"My bonus was gone when Baltimore brought me to the big camp. Everyone was telling me how great my career was going to be, but I didn't have a dime. You know what it's like, nothing until you start the season and you're trying to live on a couple of bucks a day." I did know the feeling since every player of this era had been put in the same position. Only the few who had enough bonus money to survive between paychecks avoided these pressures. There was a prolonged silence before Steve spoke.

"There were a couple of fans who hung around the hotel lobby and they always wanted to go out drinking. I never had to pay for anything and sometimes we went to Miami Beach. They knew everybody no matter where we went and I never had to worry about paying".

"One night I complained about not having any money because my bonus was gone and we didn't get paid until the start of the season. They were great guys and understanding about my problems. I was really drunk when the big guy offered to "loan me a bunch of money". Steve couldn't remember how much, but it was obvious the sum was large.

"When I asked, how long do I have to repay, the answer was not to worry about it." "We really like you and just want to help out. Somewhere down the road you can pay us back. You're going to be making a lot of money and when you feel comfortable about repaying, just let us know. There are no strings attached". The mob had found Steve and he accepted their offer.

Once Dalkowski unburdened himself he lowered his head to the bar and cried non stop for five minutes, his arms providing a shield. The bartender moved toward us but stopped when I waved him away. For all he knew, it could have been an emotional moment between two lovers and not a time to interrupt. The information was dynamic and possibly the missing piece of the puzzle as to what happened to the talent that no one else ever had.

Steve's last game in Lewiston produced velocity on his fastball approaching earlier years and Ripken commented on this while we were dressing after the game. Skills diminished by age or injury can't be recovered, but Dalkowski was throwing near 100 mph or greater. Alcohol may have offered a release of his fears.

A few weeks before the end of our season Steve showed up again, this time asking me to come to his apartment after the game. I agreed since I could leave at any time knowing he would be safe when I left. There was an unexpected, pleasant surprise when the door opened after ringing the buzzer. "Hi Tim, Steve told me you were coming over". This welcoming person was young and attractive.

Dalkowski had charmed someone with a sizable trust fund to be his companion. It became obvious I was entering her apartment as there were feminine touches to the decorating producing a warm atmosphere. The idea something might go awry over the next several hours seemed to be improbable. "Slim, what the hell do you want to do?" There was something on my mind and maybe he could help.

"Dalko, we're leaving for Reno tomorrow and I've always wanted to know how to play craps but don't have a clue." "Slim, don't worry, you've come to a master and when you hit the tables there will be a fortune to be made!" Magically, a pair of dice appeared and our game board was the back wall of the dinette area, after the furniture had been moved to the living room. Our hostess dissolved into the background and we devoted ourselves to my crash course.

Steve and I were so intent, few drinks were consumed and conversation was related to my goal. We were having a great time together without discussing baseball. But once he tired of this activity, Dalkowski reverted to form and heavy drinking started. Within thirty minutes he went over the edge and became abusive, as I had anticipated.

"Let's get serious about this shit and play some black jack. You just came over here to kick my ass and make me look bad in front of my woman.!" Since I wasn't surprised as to this turn it was easy to adapt. "Get the cards out and let's get it on."

This was the one game I understood and it would be fun to play with monopoly money just to test our skill levels. We switched from dealer to player whenever a black jack occurred. Our fake money grew in front of me the longer we played. I was playing cards with skill and since it was a single deck, it was easy to card count and improve my odds. Steve was drunk and getting angrier by the minute as my winnings increased. After winning another hand Dalkowski shouted an order. "Get your ass over here with the checkbook"!

Even though we had agreed to the play money format, Dalkowski somehow arrived at a $300 debt owed to me. "Steve, I don't want your money"! This wasn't good enough for him and his friend was directed to write a check for that amount, without question. Now he was comfortable and offered a warm goodbye for the last time. I slipped the check back to his lady as I left their apartment.

Every year it became more difficult to find teammates who knew the Dalkowski story, let alone his name. Steve was gone and a black hole swallowed his fame from almost a decade before. I became aware of his whereabouts in the late 1970's through the efforts of Mark Fleisher. Mark was my best friend in college, hired by the Elmira Star Gazette as a sports writer just after my career ended. His journalistic skills were incredible and should have been showcased in a larger market. But he chose to stay in Elmira and raise a family away from big city problems.

"Tim, I've located Dalkowski and will be doing a major story for the paper. I need some background and fill since you two were close. There is so little out there about this guy, I think this would be a great opportunity for everyone who saw him in Elmira to understand more about his problems". We both didn't know there were several high profile publications doing exactly the same thing.

Mark's article hit the wire services and because it was so well written, garnered him an AP writing award in New York Sports reporting. The article was published June 17, 1979, in the Star Gazette. The importance of mentioning the date is in relation to Dalkowski's current, admitted, almost total memory loss of his playing days due to the effects of alcohol abuse.

Fleisher's research and contact with Steve provided both accurate and amusing anecdotes directly from the source. He perfectly blended what I had provided, along with Dalkowski's still fresh memories. This included a question as to whether his fastball had ever been clocked in any manner and the answer was no. This is part of the story that best describes the person and baseball innocence of the time.

"One spring, Dalkowski's Miami hotel room was next to Miss Ecuador's during the Miss Universe competition. He bought a hand drill, bored a hole in the wall and provided teammates with a narration of what was going on. Within a few days, the walls resembled a hunk of Swiss cheese. Eventually, the peepholes were discovered and Oriole manger Paul Richards gave Dalkowski the tongue-lashing of the century".

"Baseball men still talk about 1960 when he fanned 262 batters at Stockton in the California League. Trouble was, Dalkowski walked 262, too. He fanned 24 men in an Appalachian League game in 1957. He once pitched a no hitter and lost 9-8. He couldn't control his fastball or the chronic drinking problem that relegated him to a page in the trivia book. Today, Dalkowski, 40, lives quietly with his second wife and their six year old daughter in Bakersfield, California, where he works as a landscaper for Charlie Earleys Handyman Service".

Mark had done the legwork on his own to locate Steve in order to complete the story. It took a great deal of persuasion on my part to obtain Dalkowski's home phone number. Fleisher had enjoyed a decade of my stories and knew there was an honest reason for my request.

One Sunday evening, I called Bakersfield, California not knowing what I would find at the other end of the line. My call was timed so the three hour time differential might find Steve with his wife after dinner and prior to prime time television. There was an assumption on my part Sunday would be a day of rest and we would be able to renew our friendship gently.

"I'm sorry. Steve is in bed and can't talk to anyone right now". There was something wrong given the time of night and his wife wanting to hang the phone up quickly. Somehow I convinced her of my sincerity and she went to wake her husband.

The wait was at least five minutes and I could hear muffled conversation that sometimes had the tone of an argument. Steve finally answered and it was obvious he was drunk but aware of who I was and capable of carrying on a conversation.

"Slim, how the hell are ya' and why are you calling me"? Knowing there would be a retention problem I kept the answer short, briefly mentioning the article Mark had written as my reason. "Goddamn, everybody in the country has been calling me. I just got off the phone with Boog and some guy called wanting to do a movie. What the hell's going on"?

It was obvious Mark's story and another in a major publication provided enough information to track him down, just as I had done this night. The pressure was overwhelming to Steve and he had turned to his only friend, the bottle, for comfort. I wished him good luck and hung up the phone.

What started as nothing more than a reconnection to the past jolted my senses. I closed the den door and sat alone with my feelings. It didn't take long before realizing my call had furthered Steve's collapse. I knew nothing we discussed would have any influence on his future and our respective lives had to move forward.

Dalkowski became a migrant farm worker in the California fields, picking cotton, sugar beets, beans and carrots. His drink of choice was cheap wine, which he would buy when the bus stopped on the way to the crop field. Often, he would place a bottle in the next row as motivation to continue. The greatest arm in the history of professional baseball, bar none, could only measure his future by how far his glass goal was from his reach.

The June 30th, 2003 edition of Sports Illustrated was dedicated to, "Where are They Now?" The cover photo was that of Bo Jackson who had a meteoric career in both professional baseball and football. The featured people were nationally known making Dalkowski's inclusion significant. A short list featured Nancy Kerrigan, Eddie Lebaron, Jerry Lucas, and my favorite, Morganna (The Kissing Bandit).

Steve's inclusion featured a full page black and white photo showing his classic form in front of a background of typical outfield advertisements for the 1960 Stockton Port's. If Lew and Ted's Service was still in business, they received national attention along with, "Take Your Family to Church This Week". The picture was classic to use because this was the year Dalkowski struck out 262 and walked 262 in 170 innings and threw a baseball through the pictured fence on a bet. His record was 7-15 with an ERA of 5.14. The four page article was written by Pete McEntegart and conveyed the essence of the person perfectly.

"Dalkowski doesn't remember much of the next 30 years. He suffers from alcohol-related dementia, but the gaps in his memory don't start until about 1964. "I keep trying and trying to remember," he says. "But I don't". His sister, Pat Cain, can't fill in the blanks for him, because he stopped talking to his family around that same time. At some point he was married again, to a motel clerk named Virginia, though today he struggles even to recall her name. He never had children. ("Thank God," he says soberly.)

Dalkowski moved to Oklahoma City with Virginia in 1993, but when she died of a brain aneurysm in 1994, it was time for him to come home. His parents had passed away, but Cain was living in New Britain. She arranged for Dalkowski to move in the Walnut Hill Care Center, just down the hill from Dalkowski's old high school baseball field. Initially, Cain was told Dalkowski likely wouldn't live more than a year. Yet Dalkowski has rallied. Give his decades of drinking, he is remarkably healthy, and he has begun to display the easy manner his old friends remember.

Sitting with his family and friends in the stands after throwing the first pitch at the Rock Cats game, he mugs good-naturedly with this three-year old grandniece, Samantha. He sings along with God Bless America during the seventh-inning stretch. Yet it's the game that interests him most. When a New Britain pitcher gets two strikes on a batter, Dalkowski says, "Let it all hang out." Dalkowski can no longer let it all hang out, yet he finally seems to be keeping it together."

Once a person becomes legendary there are untruths repeated over time, building energy, until the real story is lost and they become fact. The internet has become the standard for research and once something is logged in it is available for repeating whether it is correct or not. The most reported and repeated has Steve being the model for Tim Robbins character, Nuke Laloosh, in Ron Shelton's classic movie, "Bull Durham". The real character was probably a combination of Dalkowski and Greg Arnold.

Greg was a wild right hander who played a guitar and drove a red sports car, same as Nuke. Steve was a left hander who couldn't carry a note let alone play the guitar and didn't have a driver's license because of his drinking problem. Arnold and Shelton playing together four seasons makes sense to me. Dalkowski was long gone before Shelton signed and word of mouth stories about Steve were a decade old. Arnold fits the description of Nuke far better than Dalkowski but Shelton probably blended the two together for his character. Shortly after the release of the film, USA Today ran a major story on the speculation Arnold was the model. Their conclusions were the same as mine.

The most blatant abuse of the truth can be found on the website, www.sportshollywood.com. "One of his wilder pitches hit an announcer—up in the announcer's booth, and he finished one season at Stockton with 262 strikeouts and 262 walks. Writer/director Ron Shelton was playing on that team with Dalkowski in 1960, and he used the announcer incident and these exact statistics in his screenplay for Bull Durham. He used Dalkowski as the model for the films character Nuke Laloosh". In 1960 Shelton might have been old enough to be the bat boy since his professional debut in the Orioles system wasn't until 1966.

Recently, Keith Olbermann had a ten-minute segment on MSNBC about Steve. There was a thirty second interview where Dalkowski showed no ability to remember his past. Many incorrect stories had been prepared for the broadcast by a researcher using the internet and Olberman damaged his credibility by using the false information.

During the 2003 season, the Baltimore Orioles invited Steve to throw out a first pitch at Camden Yards. There couldn't have been one half of one percent in the stands who knew why this person was being honored. Had I known of the event, I would have been on the field to offer a handshake and hug even though he wouldn't have known me.

ONE LAST HURRAH

My career had been over for nine years when I decided to give a group of friends, including my brother in law, Joe Slavin, a taste of the major leagues and what might have been mine. Tickets were provided by the Orioles and we were staying at the visiting club's hotel, The Cross Keys Inn, in suburban Baltimore. Their best rooms were ours after my having name dropped enough during the reservation process to convince the clerk I was part of the Orioles great past. The year was 1979 and we were set for a good time and no way to know there was going to be a bonus the next morning.

Don Baylor, my roommate from a decade before, reached his zenith as a player this season and provided a genuine star for my group to meet. This was the year Don led the American League with 139 RBI's and 120 runs scored, winning the MVP award for the league along with being named to the AL all-star team. Baylor also reached the World Series three times in his career with three different teams, Boston, Minnesota and Oakland. He was selected to be the Colorado Rockies first manager and also manager of the Chicago Cubs making more than $1,000,000 per year. Our shared hotel room at the Cadillac Hotel in Rochester was only $250 per week.

The game was over quickly with Baltimore extending the Angels losing streak to five games. When we returned to the hotel there was a message from Don saying he would be late due to a business meeting. Also, there was notice his manager, Jim Fregosi, had placed a curfew on the team. Fregosi was named manager of the Angels the year before at age thirty six, replacing Dave Garcia who was fired a third of the way into the season. We only needed to find the bar at this point.

Everyone was having the great time I had planned and hoped to pull off. The atmosphere was major league from the moment we walked into the lobby and players were seen milling about. Routine stuff for me but memorable for others. Few would ever have another chance to experience such a moment in their lifetimes.

After feeling a squeeze on my left shoulder, I turned and saw Don looking down at me with a broad grin. "Roomie, how the hell are you doing? I don't have much time before curfew, introduce me to everyone". I went around the table providing short biographical sketches for all.

My enjoyment came from watching faces as they shook hands with Baylor. This proved to be my ultimate validation in front of everyone, including the one hundred plus in the bar this night.

Baylor sat at our table and we had ten minutes to catch up on our respective lives. He and I were on a roll personally, just different playing fields. Even in this short period, we had a chance to do what is best between friends and that is to reminisce. Just before the clock showed twelve, Don was gone, avoiding a $1,000 fine.

Everyone wanted to know more details about the Baylor connection and also my career. There were additional stories since the Angels had acquired four players from my past, including Bobby Grich. The combination of Grich and Baylor would produce 66 home runs and 240 RBI's on the way to the Angels winning the AL West championship.

The party was over at 2 am and time to pay the bill. A responsibility I had assumed from the beginning since I wanted no one to feel uncomfortable as to the trip's overall cost and a worry about expenditures. My foggy calculation put the bar tab at more than $200 when I called our waitress over. "Are you Mr. Sommer"? Given the time of night and circumstances, it was hard to understand how she knew my name. "Yes I am".

"Mr. Baylor has picked up your tab and has been very generous with his tip. He wanted to tell you how sorry he is there couldn't have been more time to spend with you and your friends". The first reaction to this news was not how much money had been saved, but youthful memories of a decade past in Rochester. I guided my herd to the elevators and went to bed.

The major league moment occurred the next morning when four of our group gathered for breakfast in the hotel coffee shop. Angel players were scattered about but Nolan Ryan and Rick Miller were seated directly behind us. Miller and I had played against each other in '69 and '70, but there was no recognition on his part. We all locked into Nolan's story.

"There was this game in Detroit on a Sunday afternoon with so much humidity in the air it was hard to see the signals. Warming up I was strong and the fastball was the way to start until the haze burned off. The first two I threw were down the pipe and this umpire called both balls. They weren't even questionable and after the second I knew there was something wrong. When the inning was over, we met half way up the line as I headed to the dugout. He was facing the field with his arms folded, not looking at me".

"Noly, I blew a lot of calls this inning. I was out all night, got drunk, got laid and I've had two hours sleep. You're throwing so hard, I can't focus or react fast enough to make a call. Just let me get through the next couple of innings and I'll make it up to you." I became a hero for allowing my friends to share this experience and another chance to reflect on why I chose to try and catch the baseball brass ring.

My decision to retire seemed easy when I picked up the phone and placed a call to Lou Gorman in Kansas City. I had been turned down for another local low level job and since Mary was the only bread winner, it was time to move on. Soon, I found a job in the office of a local factory making

$100 a week as a clerk. There was comfort knowing the check would be there every Friday and no yearly negotiations. I wasn't prepared for what happened over the next two weeks.

I had barely settled into a normal job routine when Lou called, offering me the minor league pitching coach job for the Royals. This was shocking since there had never been any pursuit on my part for such a position. I didn't know the friendly nurturing I offered to younger pitchers late in my career hadn't gone unnoticed by Gorman. Even though Mary gave me approval, I wasn't able to change my new mind set. Galen Cisco accepted the offer and went on to a twenty plus year career in the major leagues with several clubs.

One week later the switchboard operator paged me in the factory. "Tim, you have a call from the Kansas City Royals holding". Few in the plant knew of my background but the page caused many to gather near the phone when I answered the call.

"Tim, I know you don't have any business background but I believe you will be able to handle what I'm going to offer. Some trucking people from Oklahoma have bought our new club in Sarasota and need a general manager. They're willing to pay $300 a week based on my recommendation. You have to make up your mind in twenty four hours and then be there in the next forty eight". All the factors involved for turning down the previous offer were in place and I turned Lou down once again. This was the last time baseball came calling.

Those who have this opportunity and choose not to try will wonder the rest of their lives if they could have made it to the top, playing field or front office. Even though my pond had grown to the size of an ocean, I proved to myself I could swim with the big fish.

Made in the USA
Las Vegas, NV
27 November 2020